29.95
67c
54

D1130922

D

Controlling
the Offender in
the Community

Controlling the Offender in the Community

Reforming the Community-
Supervision Function

Todd R. Clear
Rutgers University
Vincent O'Leary
State University of New York
at Albany

LexingtonBooks
D.C. Heath and Company
Lexington, Massachusetts
Toronto

Library of Congress Cataloging in Publication Data

Clear, Todd R.
    Controlling the offender in the community.

    Includes bibliographical references and index.
    1. Community-based corrections—United States.
I. O'Leary, Vincent. II. Title.
HV9304.C58   1982   364.6′8   81-47444
ISBN 0-669-04633-7

Published simultaneously in Canada

Printed in the United States of America

International Standard Book Number: 0-669-04633-7

Library of Congress Catalog Card Number: 81-47444

To Community-Supervision Workers

Contents

Contents

Figures and Tables

Acknowledgments

Foremost among the efforts deserving recognition here are those of our research partners—the probation and parole officers who have participated in our research projects over the last decade. Their collective contribution in terms of time alone easily exceeds thousands of hours. Their contribution to the ideas expressed in this book is even greater.

Our debt extends to numerous colleagues whose work in community corrections since 1971 has influenced our thinking. Most prominent among them are Don M. Gottfredson, Andrew von Hirsch, Kathleen J. Hanrahan, S. Christopher Baird, P. Kevin Benoit, Leslie T. Wilkins, and Larry Solomon. Lawrence Travis III and James Fox provided research assistance. Margaret Zusky and Susan Lasser of Lexington Books patiently allowed us to incorporate the work of these colleagues in various drafts over a long period of writing. Janice Greene, Lucy Gedmintas, and Peggy Kuhn provided valuable assistance in typing the manuscript.

The initial stages of our work were funded through the RANN Program of the National Science Foundation, under a grant to Vincent O'Leary. Later work was made possible by grants from the National Institute of Corrections. The opinions, findings, and conclusions presented are our own and not necessarily those of the National Science Foundation or the National Institute of Corrections.

Introduction

The principles, perspectives, and models elaborated in this book represent one step in the process of changing the criminal-justice system, one contribution to a trend toward more-effective and more-just government-administered social control. We anticipate that our arguments and analyses will improve and be improved upon as our work in community supervision continues.

We began our work in 1971 in a small branch of a large metropolitan probation department. Since then, we have tested our model in over twenty different agencies, almost a dozen local projects, and three national projects. It proved conceptually sound wherever we took it. Wherever appropriate resources were provided for implementation, the changes have taken hold and reflect long-term commitments by the agencies involved using objectives-based approaches to risk control. Where implementation of change was not carefully planned or conducted, the results were less strong. From these experiences, we have learned to emphasize the importance of giving careful attention to the change process as part of any reform effort.

We have also learned the importance of having a clear conceptual basis for change efforts. By maintaining a focus on the values underlying risk control, many of the dilemmas we faced in our projects proved easier to resolve. Finally, we learned the importance of caution in the details of change. Sometimes ideas that appeared imminently reasonable simply did not work in practice. A sense of programmatic flexibility combined with a commitment to the values of risk control enabled us to complete our work.

We have organized this book to present this point of view. In part I we discuss the conceptual problems affecting community supervision, beginning with an overview chapter on the problems of community supervision. After reviewing the various contemporary rationales for punishment in chapter 2, we suggest that risk control is the appropriate aim of community supervision. In chapter 3, we describe some of the constraints that must be placed on any system of risk control, and we present some principles to serve as guidelines for controlling offenders in the community.

These principles emerged in the course of our work in probation and parole agencies. We began with a general desire to improve the effectiveness of supervision and brought to that effort certain values concerning correctional administration, discussed in chapter 2. In applying these values to operating community-supervision agencies, we came to perceive the crucial role of risk control; the importance of classifying both risk and offense seriousness in order to structure decisions; and the need for programmatic flexibility. Thus, what began as an effort at planned change in community supervision ultimately became a learning laboratory in which we could test the feasibility of various principles of constrained risk control. For example, in our initial projects, we did not have an empirically validated risk-screening instrument. Instead, we used a rather crude, subjective classification approach that combined some managerial concerns with risk-control concerns (this device is described in chapter 5). It was in using this approach that we came to understand the value of a standardized instrument for improving risk-classification reliability—too often, our own provoked disputes about the appropriate subjective classification of individual clients. More recently, we turned to objective screening devices, and the problem of classification reliability is now one of training staff to use these instruments correctly.

We also learned that the key to real change, as we have defined it in chapter 1, was to influence the cognitive processes of supervision offices in their work with clients. In the day-to-day dynamics of the office, officers come under great pressure to routinize their work, to ignore the need for risk control, and to ignore restraints on their discretionary decision making. Some mechanism for officers to resist these pressures was needed if we were ever to implement risk control in a manner consistent with the general values of justice.

In part II we describe our efforts to make risk control effective at the line level of community-supervision operations in the real world of community supervision. Chapter 4 describes the work world of supervision officers and the problems and concerns they confront in performing their work. The problem is to direct the activities of these officers toward managing the offender's risk. We also describe the projects we undertook to design and implement changes directed toward this end. Chapter 5 describes in detail the result of this work—an objectives-based case-planning process—and presents the conceptual basis for each step of the process.

Real change can occur only when all levels of an organization are making use of the risk-control approach described in part II. Objectives-based case planning can help to focus the line officer's attention on the risk-control process. However, whether the supervision effort reflects the details contained in the case plan depends largely on the way in which line staff are managed in their work. In part III we discuss the managerial/administrative aspects of risk control: how to use the information contained in case plans systematically to improve the effectiveness of community supervision.

In most agencies, management of community-supervision activities occurs at two levels. At the supervisory level, the concern is to monitor the activities of line officers, who have front-line control of discretion and implementation of risk control. In chapter 6 we describe the scope of supervisors' responsibility and show how they can use data from objectives-based case planning to make supervision of activities more effective.

At the highest, or administrative, level of management, the responsibility is to plan and evaluate supervision activities. The most critical administrative activity is to decide how to distribute organizational resources in order to achieve organizational goals. Chapter 7 describes how the use of objectives-based case-planning data can improve several recently developed administrative technologies for resource management. In the final chapter we provide some concluding observations about the implications of our work for community supervision.

Part I
Community
Supervision and
Risk Control

1 Reform and Change in Community Supervision

The Problems of Community Supervision

Corrections systems in the United States today face problems of three kinds: fiscal, technical, and conceptual. The fiscal problems are perhaps the most obvious. Under increasingly austere government budgets, corrections agencies simply lack the resources to handle all offenders in an optimum manner. Not only are basic services such as training and education programs lacking; more often than not there is also a shortage of space, professional staff, and facilities to handle the medical, housing, and other daily needs of offenders.[1] And it is unlikely that sufficient funds will become available to ameliorate these problems in the foreseeable future.

Technical problems, though less obvious, equally tax the capacity of corrections to perform its duties. On the one hand, the technologies of corrections have come under heavy criticism.[2] According to a recent two-year study by a national panel on rehabilitation:

> After 40 years of research and literally hundreds of studies, almost all of the conclusions that can be reached have to be formulated in terms of what we do not know. . . . The entire body of research appears to justify only the conclusion that we do not know of any program or method of rehabilitation that could be guaranteed to reduce the criminal activity of released offenders.[3]

If the traditional techniques of corrections are suspect, the prospects of its support technologies are even more dismal: agencies lack even rudimentarily helpful information systems, management practices, and personnel policies. With the exception of an occasional computer, the technologies of both core processes and office routines often remain those of the 1940s and 1950s.

Most difficult, however, are the conceptual contradictions now affecting the field. Despite decades of at least verbal support by corrections officials for the value of rehabilitation and a philosophic trend toward more humane attitudes toward offenders, recently there has been an almost wholesale rejection of offender-oriented corrections. Although the courts have consistently broadened legal protection of the convicted,[4] the most effective political voices seem to belong to those who emphasize incapacitative goals and whose ideas of justice minimize the notion of corrections.[5] In neither the judicial nor the political sphere does the offender's need for services appear to be a central concern. Many operational changes are occurring: parole has been abolished,[6] prisons have been declared unconstitutional,[7] jails closed,[8] mandatory sentencing schemes enacted,[9] incarceration alternatives developed,[10] and new institutions are being built.[11] But there is no unified theme or direction to these changes. Corrections systems appear to have no clear purpose or function, but seem instead simply to respond to pressures from the environment. No central rationale exists to help officials or policymakers select among alternative long-range policies and actions.

These three difficulties are linked, of course: restricted or reduced budgets contribute to the technically outmoded operation of the agencies. But most important, the failure to establish a comprehensive conceptual framework exacerbates the difficulty of using fiscal resources efficiently to develop and apply new technologies.

The problems confronting community supervision are products of those affecting the entire field of offender management. Thus, resolution of existing difficulties in community supervision will require stability in the larger correctional context. Although the focus of this book is the management of offenders who live in the community while being punished, our comments about community supervision also apply to the corrections system as a whole.

As we use it, the term *community supervision* includes all programs for managing the offender while he or she is serving some portion of a sentence in the community. Thus, it includes not only the traditional agencies of probation and parole, but also settings such as halfway houses and furlough programs. Our focus on community supervision is a product not only of our personal values, but also of our belief that solving the problems identified above will ultimately require greater use of community-based sanctions. For one thing, community supervision costs less in terms of tax dollars than incarceration and therefore represents a more fiscally responsible approach to corrections. It also offers a partial solution to the technical and conceptual problems of corrections. This book presents a model for resolving these issues as they pertain to community supervision. First, we argue that the primary purpose of community supervision is risk control—minimizing the probability that an offender will commit a new offense while being punished in the community. Second, we argue that risk control and the techniques chosen to achieve it are constrained by general notions of justice based on the nature of the offense. Finally, we demonstrate how an objectives-based approach to supervision provides the foundation for improving the risk-control actions taken in community-supervision agencies by line officers, immediate line supervisors, and agency administators. That is, these technologies, employed systematically at all levels of the community-supervision agency, can integrate staff functions while focusing them on the purpose of risk control.

We do not claim that this model provides a definitive resolution of all the issues and problems of community supervision. We do believe it can increase the viability of community supervision as a fiscally responsible, increasingly effective and purposeful criminal sanction, and that it will stimulate additional thought and, perhaps, solutions to the problems facing corrections and community supervision.

Organizational Change or System Reform?

Much of the current debate about community supervision appears to involve a false choice between organizational change and system reform. Advocates of the former argue that community supervision must focus on implementing new strategies for handling offenders, ranging from more-effective surveillance to better information systems to more-appropriate interventions.[12] The major concern of this group is organizational practices. Those who press for reform, on the other hand, maintain that mere organizational changes are not enough; instead, the very purposes and even availability of the community sanction must be altered. Proponents of system reform would restrict the capacity of supervision officers to enforce technical conditions, or even abolish compulsory supervision and replace it with a voluntary "service" of corrections.[13]

We believe that any effort to restructure supervision must address system reform and organizational change equally. Changes in administrative or treatment procedures will not be useful without clarification of the purpose of supervision. Similarly, the effectiveness of any comprehensive reform of community supervision will ultimately depend on the manner in which it is implemented as a change.

That change and reform are interrelated is confirmed by such efforts in other settings. For example, many attempts to reform sentencing procedures through the implementation of guidelines have failed to influence judicial sentences, partly because they did not also alter existing organizational norms.[14] Likewise, several attempts to implement diversion programs as organizational changes have proved unsuccessful, partly because they were not accompanied by attempts to reform overall sentencing practices and thus ensure that decision makers would actually use the alternatives.[15] Organizational change and system reform are mutually supportive aspects of any attempt to improve corrections significantly. Reform efforts begin with a rethinking of the conceptual basis for the tasks being addressed. Change efforts are concerned with developing the procedures and practices that make reform actually occur. In both cases the intention is to translate goals into actions, and each level of analysis is not only valid—it is absolutely necessary if the efforts are to take effect.

Two Approaches to Translating Goals into Actions

Most reform efforts take a deductive approach to change, establishing broad principles of reform first and then general parameters and specific procedures. In the movement to rethink the rationale for sentencing offenders, for example, the new retributionist school first defines the broad principle of desert, then establishes the general parameters of commensurability and parsimony, and finally provides specific examples of approved sanctions under this model.[16]

Experience shows that such a linear approach is well suited to describe and justify a reform effort but is frequently inadequate for actually implementing reform. For example, determinate-sentencing legislation in Maine, Indiana, California, and New Jersey has resulted in harsher penalties, usually broader discretion, and hidden utilitarian values contrary to the very principles that provided so much of the rhetorical support for change. Similarly, in preparing a recent report on presumptive sentencing, staff members expressed strongly divergent positions on how to make operational a previously agreed-upon series of principles and general parameters.[17]

There is an important distinction between defining or justifying reform efforts and implementing the changes needed to produce those reforms. To be persuasive, reform efforts must be presented in linear logic. Indeed, the following chapters provide a linear exposition on the need for reforming community supervision. Implementation strategies, however, though they must be carefully planned, cannot be linear if they are to be successful. Once the broad principles of the reform are defined, effort must turn to restructuring the activities of criminal-justice workers to make them congruent with those principles. Once the specific procedural changes are defined, the general parameters to guide and reinforce the principles can be outlined in terms of how they logically support the specific intentions and general purposes. In the case of sentencing-reform efforts, the first step would be to define and justify the broad principle; then the change effort would begin, in the form of designing and instituting specific procedures for bringing sentencing practices into line with that principle. From the act of changing sentencing practices, the general parameters to reinforce those practices would emerge, and both reform and change would have occurred. In this organic approach to innovation, the principles reinforcing the innovation emerge as a result of a general reform effort.

Accordingly, the work reported in this book proceeded from two initial assumptions: that certain management principles and correctional values, described in detail in the next two chapters, ought to guide decision making in community supervision; and that the primary function of supervision is to control the risk posed by the offender. We then turned our attention to the line-supervision officer, to identify ways to implement these principles in day-to-day supervision. During this lengthy process, we gained a special understanding of the officer's work in supervising offenders. From this understanding we derived an objectives-based system of supervision as the mechanism for implementing risk control. The use of this supervision system led us to identify operational parameters for managing risk-control efforts in the community. This organic model for correctional innovations is preferable to the more widely used linear one. In giving equal emphasis simultaneously to alterning the activities of community-supervision staff and the purposes those activities serve, it differs from a number of other current attempts to reformulate the field of community supervision.[18]

Promoting Real Change

An organic approach avoids the pitfall of most change efforts in human-service organizations. Too often, procedures, titles, or paper policies are modified while work at the line level continues unaffected. The difficulty of any change effort—and the underlying goal of pursuing change and reform simultaneously—is to change actual performance methods instead of merely changing the rules or paperwork that surround the work as it is being done. Even in the face of legislative changes, for example, trial judges often continue to take actions in court that maintain past norms and reflect their own values.[19] The Supreme Court's holding in *Miranda* has been subverted by the practices of line police officers.[20] It is a small wonder, then, that virtually every community-supervision worker can tell of major alterations in agency procedures that had little or no effect on the way staff actually handled clients.

Real change means that line officers perform their work in ways that are consistent with the goals of the change *and* without unanticipated, negative side effects. The requirement of additional paperwork to do case planning, for example, may ultimately reduce the quantity (and, unintentionally, the quality) of line interaction with clients. Therefore, one test of any real change in government services is whether it significantly alters specific work activities at the line level. A second, related test is whether the goals of the change are achieved. If the activities that constitute the government service are never altered, is unlikely that the goals have changed in any operational sense.

A final test of real change is that it not produce the very consequences it was designed to avert. For example, diversion programs have been justified on the grounds that they will reduce the number of people processed by criminal-justice agencies, but some evaluations have found that these programs have in fact increased the number of people taken into the system.[21]

This criterion establishes a strong case for closely monitoring the implementation of any change effort flowing from reform goals. Locating and exposing a criminal justice (or community-supervision) problem is relatively easy; doing something about it in the day-to-day operational context is substantially more difficult.

Three Principles for Reform and Change

There are three overriding principles that, when applied to efforts to implement changes and reforms, help prevent unintentional, negative consequences.

Controlling the Net

Change efforts ought to be directed toward reducing rather than increasing social control. There is no objective evidence that augmenting social control through criminal justice increases the stability of society. On the contrary, the United States punishes a higher proportion of people more severely in more repressive facilities than any other Western society.[22] Yet the nation's crime problem continues to be a source of deep social conflict. For a reform to be logically related to the problems of criminal justice in this country, it must not produce an increase in the behaviors prohibited or numbers processed by the formal social-control network.

There is a more important reason for not expanding the net of social control. Beyond the fact that more criminal-justice involvement has not had an appreciable impact on the so-called crime problem, recent budget allocations to crime-fighting agencies have diverted resources from other legitimate government aims that are certainly humane and may ultimately have more ir .ct on levels of crime, such as reducing unemployment and improving the quality of life in our cities. Major reductions in the extent of crime will not be achieved through enlargement of the criminal-justice system, nor is expansion of the system fiscally or conceptually sound. Instead, changes in any area of criminal justice ought to concentrate resources on the most serious types of offenses and offenders.

Guaranteeing Due Process

The uniqueness of the U.S. criminal-justice system resides in its provision of rights to all citizens. One of the responsibilities of criminal-justice agencies is to protect those rights by developing meaningful policies that reinforce due process. In recent years, many criminal-justice agencies have resisted the steady trend toward more effective due-process guarantees in all justice practices. It has fallen largely to the courts to protect these rights and extend them to the various justice operations. A strong emphasis on due-process rights provides justice agencies with public credibility. These agencies are therefore responsible for pursuing reforms and changes that are not only consistent with due process, but actually promote it.

Sustaining the Capacity for Change

It is clear that no uniform answers now exist for the improvement of either justice or crime control. One reason is that the improvement of criminal justice is a developmental process, so that any changes undertaken must be designed to facilitate the future reforms that will necessarily follow. No new policy or approach is in any sense final; history shows the field to be dynamic, providing for steadily (if slowly) improving approaches to justice. Thus, any change undertaken should recognize the necessity—indeed, the inevitability—of future changes. Reformers should pave the way for future improvements by maintaining flexibility.

Using these three principles as guides can help ensure that reforms and changes in community corrections will not reduce the quality of correctional practice by producing unintended consequences, and instead may make operations more purposeful.

Notes

1. For one summary of shortcomings in corrections facilities and programs, see Gail S. Funke, *An Analysis of Costs of Correctional Standards for New Jersey* (Washington, D.C.: Correctional Economics Center, 1978).

2. See, for example, Douglas Lipton, Robert Martinson, and Judith Wilks, *The Effectiveness of Correctional Treatment* (New York: Praeger, 1975).

3. Lee Sechrest et al., *The Rehabilitation of Criminal Offenders: Problems and Prospects* (Washington, D.C.: National Academy of Sciences, 1979), p. 3.

4. See Sol Rubin, *The Law of Criminal Correction* (St. Paul: West, 1973).

5. See Ernest van den Haag, *Punishing Criminals: On an Old and Painful Question* (New York: Basic Books, 1975); and David Fogel, *". . . we are the Living Proof . . .": The Justice Model for Corrections* (Cincinnati: Anderson, 1975).

6. See *Maine Revised Statutes Annotated*, titles 16, 17, 17-A (1975); and *The Indiana Penal Code*, secs. 35, 36 (1976).

7. Holt v. Sarver, 309 F. Supp. 362 (E.D. Ark. 1970).

8. Jones v. Wittenberg, 323 F. Supp. 93 (N.D. Ohio 1971).

9. See, for example, Association of the Bar of New York City, *The Nation's Toughest Drug Law: Evaluating the New York Experience* (New York, 1977).

10. See, for example, National Institute of Corrections, *1982 Program Plan* (Washington, D.C., 1981).

11. Milton G. Rector, "Optimism for the 1980s" (Paper presented at a meeting of the American Probation and Parole Association, Niagara Falls, Canada, October 27, 1980).

12. Walter Barkdull, "Probation: Call It Control—and Mean It," *Federal Probation* 40 (1976):3-8; S. Christopher Baird, "Probation and Parole Classification: The Wisconsin Model," *Corrections Today*, May/June 1981:36-41; Gary Arling and Ken Lerner, *Client Management Classification* (Washington, D.C.: National Institute of Corrections, 1981).

13. Andrew von Hirsch and Kathleen J. Hanrahan, *The Question of Parole: Retention, Reform, or Abolition?* (Cambridge, Mass.: Ballinger, 1979); David T. Stanley, *Prisoners among Us: The Problem of Parole* (Washington, D.C.: Brookings Institution, 1976).

14. See William D. Rich et al., *Sentencing by Mathematics: An Evaluation of Sentencing Guidelines in Three Courts* (Williamsburg, Va.: forthcoming); also Todd R. Clear et al., "The Middle Third of Guidelines Evaluation: From Multiple-Regression to Sentencing Reform" (Paper presented at the meeting of the American Society of Criminology, Philadelphia, November 1980).

15. Yitzak Bakal, ed., *Closing Correctional Institutions* (Lexington Books, Lexington, Mass.: D.C. Heath and Company, 1974).

16. See, for example, Andrew von Hirsch, *Doing Justice* (New York: Hill and Wang, 1976).

17. Twentieth Century Fund Task Force on Criminal Sentencing, *Fair and Certain Punishment* (New York: McGraw-Hill, 1976).

18. For examples of activity-focused approaches, see S. Christopher Baird, "Model Classification Systems in Probation and Parole," *Corrections Magazine*, May/June 1981, pp. 4-6; for examples of purpose-oriented approaches, see von Hirsch and Hanrahan, *The Question of Parole*; and David Fogel, "The Mission of Probation," mimeographed (University of Illinois-Chicago Circle, 1981).

19. See Rich et al., *Sentencing by Mathematics*, especially ch. 4.

20. Peter W. Lewis and Harry E. Allen, "Participating Miranda," *Crime and Delinquency* 23 (1977):75.

21. Franklin E. Zimring, "Measuring the Impact of Pre-Trial Diversion from the Criminal Justice System," *University of Chicago Law Review* 31 (May 1974):241.

22. Irvin Waller and Janet Chan, "Prison Use: A Canadian and International Comparison," *Criminal Law Quarterly* 17 (1974-75):47-71.

2 The Purposes of Community Supervision

To improve community supervision, we must first understand the rationale for its existence, its intended mission. Vague allusions to public protection, rehabilitation, reintegration are no longer sufficient. A specific statement of purpose with express assumptions, limitations, and prerogatives is required.

This is necessary for several reasons. First, prisons and jails are filled to capacity nationwide and states and localities are being forced to undertake costly building programs to deal with the mounting numbers of incarcerated offenders. Such facilities are increasingly expensive to erect and to operate. Given the fact that the United States incarcerates a much larger percentage of its offenders than perhaps any other Western democracy, the need for an effective system of community supervision in which the public has confidence has never been more apparent.

Second, paradoxically, at the moment that community supervision is needed most, there is an increasing trend toward reduced expenditures on human services, including corrections, at all levels of government. This trend forces administrators to restrict the scope and variety of services their organizations can continue to provide to potential clients. In times of economic growth, organizations can survive the ill effects of vagueness of purpose—indeed, growth may mute awareness of problems. Shrinking resources, however, compel administrators to reconsider their operational activities.[1] The first step in doing so is to secure an unambiguous idea of the purposes an organization serves and of their relative priority so that limited resources can be focused on the most important.[2] These general difficulties apply to all community-supervision organizations currently facing cutbacks in funding.

Third, there has been a growing dissatisfaction with the traditional activities of criminal-justice agencies and particularly with the values underlying those activities. In the last decade, criticisms of law enforcement,[3] court decision making (especially sentencing),[4] parole release and supervision,[5] corrections generally,[6] and civil commitment as an alternative to a criminal sentence have mounted.[7] Given these critical reviews of the criminal-justice system, it is appropriate to begin a consideration of a segment of that system by clarifying its aims.

In this chapter, we discuss the proper aims of criminal law and how community supervision might serve those aims. We conclude that the most legitimate model for community supervision is what might be called *con-*

strained risk control and outline some of the issues that must be addressed under that approach.

Traditional Purposes

Traditionally, the purpose of community supervision has been described as protection of the public and rehabilitation of the offender. The vagueness of this definition allows for conflicting emphases: some professionals stress community protection, while others focus on providing services to the offender. The result is a wide divergence of operations ranging from surveillance through service activities, all justified by the same statement of purpose. In a characteristic manipulation, supervision is alleged to "protect the public by rehabilitating the offender," as if other public-protection activities (such as surveillance or a return to custody) were not also legitimate aspects of community supervision.

One reason for the popularity of this vague statement of purpose appears to have been the traditional emphasis on casework as the primary technology of community supervision.[8] As originally borrowed from the social-work profession, casework meant provision of support services, including referral, welfare, training, and employment as means of improving an individual's social functioning.[9] When Freudian psychoanalysis began to influence the social-work profession by reducing the emphasis on direct services and increasing the role of analytical counseling, this development also carried over into corrections. In the field of community supervision, it meant that probation and parole officers increasingly defined their function in terms of providing therapy, with offenders' emotions being the target of concern.[10]

But a critical difference exists between traditional social-work roles and community supervision. In the latter context, the offender does not request the service voluntarily; involvement is required by law. Some writers have contended the authority with which the community-supervision officer is inevitably invested does not interfere with the relationship necessary to achieve rehabilitation: "The use of authority is not antagonistic to the principles of good social work or counseling. Further, the actual employment of authority itself . . . can be a powerful therapeutic tool."[11] This description of authority conjures a vision of legitimate influence based on the worker's recognized and accepted competence—what Yelaja calls "psychological authority."[12] In reality, the authority of corrections workers is vested in the potential raw power of the law and not necessarily in role credibility. Moreover, this type of authority is not simply a tool of the supervision officer to "serve the purpose of therapy or control;"[13] it is a fundamental manifestation of the coercive character of community supervision, which "permeates the relationship."[14]

The most problematic aspect of the protection/rehabilitation dichotomy, then, is the semantic manipulation that permits the pretense that the community-supervision officer can be both a disinterested helper dispensing therapy and a state-employed controller protecting the public. In reality, it is difficult to balance these roles. Only when both the law as a behavioral standard and the officer as a person have credibility ("rational authority"[15]) for a specific offender is such integration possible. Otherwise, in handling a case the supervision officer often finds it necessary to choose between acting as a representative of the state or serving as a therapist for the client. The recent development of the "offender-advocate" approach exacerbates this problem.

The clear and proper role of the officer in relation to offenders can flow only from an understanding of the purpose of supervision, not from a semantic manipulation. To begin resolving these difficulties, we review the traditional justifications of punishment.

Justifications of Punishment

Like other penal sanctions established by the criminal law, community supervision must be considered a punishment. Whether it is seen as lenient or severe, it restricts freedom and makes certain offender behaviors compulsory. As a punishment, it occurs in the context of one or more of the traditional justifications: retribution, general deterrence, incapacitation, and rehabilitation.

Retribution

Retribution, the classical justification of punishment, is described as nonutilitarian because it rejects the legitimacy of allowing the so-called future benefits of punishment such as the prevention or control of crime to justify the imposition of punishment:

> Benefits, such as the rehabilitation of offenders, the protection of society . . . or, even more, the deterrence of others are welcome, of course. But they are not necessary—nor are they sufficient—for punishment, and they are altogether irrelevant to making punishment just.[16]

Retributive punishment is justifiable simply and precisely because a person has offended against the legal requirements of a society. In these terms, punishment is a means of reaffirming the social order and giving credibility to the social contract. According to John Rawls, the purpose of the criminal law is to uphold basic natural duties, those which forbid us to injure other persons in their life and limb, or to deprive them of their liberty and property, and punishments are to serve this end. They are not simply a scheme of taxes and burdens designed to put a price on certain forms of conduct and in this way to guide men's conduct for mutual advantage.[17]

This view of retribution is not the same as the common belief that the offender must pay a debt to society; the debt is owed in reverse: "Laws threaten, or promise, punishment for crimes, society has obligated itself by threatening. It owes the carrying out of its threats."[18]

The principle of retribution has recently been translated into a system of penal sanctions called commensurate desert, which requires that "similar acts must be dealt with by similar measures" and that "the severity of the sentence should be related to the amount of harm done by the offense."[19] Therefore, retributionists have supported recent sentencing reforms that limit the applicability of community supervison and establish an exact penalty at the time of sentencing.[20]

Retributionists may have underestimated the potential role of community supervison in desert-oriented schemes. To the degree that community supervision involves coerced compliance with legally mandated restrictions on liberty, it is clearly retribution for an offense. If imprisonment reaffirms the social contract by denying the offender his or her freedom, then so can the lesser restrictions on liberty imposed through community supervison.

Unfortunately, the potential significance of community supervision as an alternative method of punishment is undermined by the unjustifiably long prison sentences mandated by most state penal laws. In this context, it is often difficult to perceive a sentence of probation as a punishment. The sentences provided by most codes are not only much longer than in other Western democracies,[21] but the magnitude of the penalties often makes prosecutors reluctant to ask for the maximum penalty,[22] and parole is widely used to reduce unwieldy sentences. The result is a system of make-believe penalties that undermines the legitimate symbolic significance of the penalties imposed for felonies.

Given the recognition as a punitive measure that it deserves, community supervision has the potential to serve retributive ends, through conditions such as reporting requirements and restrictions on travel. Restitution (that is, requiring the offender to "pay" for his offense through money or service to the victims or the community) as a condition of probation is another means of meeting the aims of commensurate desert. Moreover, the number, type, and duration of restrictions and/or the amount of restitution can be varied to reflect the seriousness of the offense.[23] Far from being an alternative to punishment, community supervision—if properly used—is indeed restrictive and potentially punitive. Proponents of punishment recognized this potential by providing for "community punishment" alternatives in their schemes.[24]

General Deterrence

Deterrence, the oldest utilitarian—that is, crime-control—rationale for punishment, is generally attributed to Jeremy Bentham. It consists in distributing penalties among lawbreakers in such a way as to convince the law-abiding to continue not to offend. Thus, punishment "serves to deter potential offenders by inflicting suffering on actual ones. . . . The technique works by threat . . . and we punish only that the technique may retain some effectiveness in the future."[25] General deterrence differs from specific deterrence, which consists in applying a penalty sufficient to convince the *convicted offender* not to offend again. The latter is more consistent with the concept of rehabilitation, discussed below. In its general sense, deterrence is identical to Packer's definition of the function of the criminal law: "the singular power of the criminal law resides . . . not in its coercive effect on those caught in its toils, but rather in its effect on the rest of us."[26] It is argued that deterrence is effective even for seemingly nonrational offenses. "Prospective offenders need to be no more rational than rats are when taught by means of rewards or punishments to run a maze. . . ."[27] Moreover, sanctions deter offenses by setting a moral tone and defining a moral order that, when accepted by citizens, guides their conduct.[28] Nor does deterrence seek extremely severe sanctions for offenders. As Andenaes has pointed out, "It was never a principle of criminal justice that crime should be prevented at all costs. Ethical and social considerations will always determine which measures are considered 'proper.' "[29]

The effectiveness of a deterrence-based system does depend, however, on the certainty and severity of the response to a criminal act;[30] and evidence increasingly indicates that the former may be more important than the latter.[31] Yet limitations on the ability to apprehend violators may seriously restrict the capacity to increase certainty.

As in the case of retribution, the discrepancy between inordinately severe penalties in U.S. penal codes and much lighter actual sentences reduces the deterrent potential of community-based punishment. In a recent survey of empirical deterrence research, for example, Tullock pointed out that most of the researchers counted reported crimes resulting in imprisonment as "punishment," and all others (including convictions leading to probation) as "no punishment."[32] Among many other difficulties affecting its validity, this sort of approach confuses the certainty of punishment with what is in fact a measure of its severity. There is little question that offenders who are on probation or parole feel punished.

For one thing, the very activities of apprehension and conviction have some deterrent effect independent of the severity of punishment. Moreover, the belief that community supervision (early parole or probation status) is not punitive is rooted in a naive understanding of the activity. In reality, the restrictions on liberty associated with the status of offenders in the community may well be sufficiently undesirable to deter a substantial portion of would-be offenders. The additional deterrence provided by prison penalties is suspect and probably measurable only when it involves lengthy and costly sentences.

The ultimate issue, though, is how much punishment is enough. Theoretically, it is possible to increase deterrence by increasing all punishments to life imprisonment, but aside from the intolerable financial costs and rapidly diminishing returns involved, the penalties would simply be too extreme. Community supervision, particularly probation, probably provides a level of deterrence appropriate to a vast majority of criminal offenses and offenders. Similarly, although applying uniform prison sentences might increase deterrence, in most instances such penalties cannot be justified in terms of the punishment imposed and the uncertain marginal gain in crime reduction. The use of incarceration as a marginally greater deterrent has more legitimacy when applied to serious felonies that result in serious harm to individuals and where retributive values suggest a more severe sanction.

Incapacitation

Incapacitation has recently grown in popularity as a justification for punishment, based on the rationale that punishment should be designed to make a convicted offender unable to commit another crime. Incapacitation approaches vary in focus from a desire to halt all criminal offenses to targeting only those cases involving risk of actual physical harm to others.[33] They also vary in their inclusion of risk-reduction activities. Thus, one variant of incapacitation, "social defense," advocates

> a system which aims not at punishing fault . . . but at protecting society against criminal acts . . . by means of a body of measures that are . . . designed to neutralize the offender, either by his removal or segregation, or by applying remedial or educational methods.[34]

A basic component of any incapacitation system is a risk-prediction and monitoring technology that will identify those who must be incapacitated and determine when the risk is abated sufficiently to end the control measures. Unfortunately, most researchers believe there has been "a failure to develop methodologically acceptable means of predicting dangerousness."[35]

Neither a panoply of treatment programs nor a viable prediction model is necessary to establish an incapacitative system, however. In fact, for James Q. Wilson, it is in part the failure of *both* treatment and prediction that justifies an incapacitative model:

> Society at a minimum must be able to protect itself from dangerous offenders. . . . It is a frank admission that society really does not know how to do much else. The purpose of isolating—or, more accurately, closely supervising—offenders is obvious: whatever they may do when they are released, they cannot harm society while confined or closely supervised.[36]

This point of view tends to regard all offenders as potential repeaters, and its use of cohort studies of offenders generally supports this idea.[37] As a result, those supporting an incapacitation approach typically recommend some form of imprisonment for virtually all offenders and particularly lengthy terms for violent ones.

Because incapacitation strategies often suggest severe sanctions, discussions often raise the issue of what value to assign to liberty. Some argue that the convicted offender has sufficiently proved a propensity to offend and is therefore subject to stringent incapacitation measures. Other writers maintain that since "the state is obligated to observe strict parsimony in intervening in convicted offenders' lives,"[38] it must "make the . . . incapacitation 'measure' as non-punitive as possible."[39] The latter position would limit the state to the least-intrusive measure necessary to achieve the incapacitative goal.

All forms of incapacitation arguments pose a final moral problem: punishment is administered not for what the offender has done, but for what he or she is believed likely to do in the future. This problem raises the question to what degree a free society can tolerate such extensive state power, particularly given the potential for errors.

In community supervision, an incapacitative function has long been associated with the surveillance responsiblities of the supervision officer. Some writers have questioned whether such activities in practice substantially reduce the offender's potential for criminal conduct. Working from the results of a time-motion study of federal probation officers, one research report estimated that actual contact between the officer and the client could occur only "at the rate of three minutes per week."[40] A similar study of Georgia parole caseloads resulted in a more liberal estimate of eight minutes per offender per week.[41] Neither figure argues well for the control potential of the average probation or parole officer; Stanley has concluded that:

> a parolee determined to make it does not need surveillance; a parolee determined to con his parole officer, evade him, or engage in illicit activities can find ways to do so. A parolee who is not committed either way may be induced to accept guidance and help.[42]

Some organizations have responded to this problem by requiring much higher levels of contact between a small subgroup of selected parolees and probationers at the expense of even less contact with the majority of clients.

Besides traditional surveillance, community supervision can impose a variety of incapacitative conditions, including requirements of periodic submission to urinalysis for drug use, limitations on the possession of firearms, and suspension of Fourth Amendment rights. All these common conditions of supervision aim to restrict the potential for repeated violations of the law.

The use of such conditions has raised questions regarding propriety: Can a general list of conditions be applied to all offenders undergoing community supervision, or must each specific condition be justifiably related to preventing recurrence of the crime for which the person was convicted? How intrusive may conditions be? Although substantial latitude exists for judges and agencies to apply conditions, there is a slow trend toward limiting their generality and intrusiveness.[43]

Rehabilitation

As used here, rehabilitation is a change in the offender's attitude, produced by the state's intervention due to his criminal conviction and resulting in a willingness to refrain from criminal acts. A number of aspects of that intervention could motivate the decision to refrain: fear of being caught and punished again; insight into emotional causes of criminal behavior; or access to socially legitimate opportunities as a result of learning skills while being punished. The key requirements are that the offender *choose* to refrain from new crimes (rather than being unable to, which is an incapacitative concept) and that the nature and extent of intervention have been selected precisely to influence the offender in making that choice.

Rehabilitation relies on a rationale that might best be described as individualized punishment. The earliest bases for this approach were the writings of so-called positivists, who maintained that there were innate physical differences for certain types of offenders. Later, theories based on physical differences "fell into disrepute and were replaced by somewhat more sohpisticated and empirically-based theories asserting that mental deficiency or emotional aberration constituted the predilections of criminal behavior."[44] This perspective views crime "as symptomatic of an underlying disorder. . . . one must understand and treat the underlying condition and not merely its symptoms."[45]

Recently the focus has shifted again, to identifying societal/environmental characteristics, such as differential opportunity structures, that make crime-free living difficult for individual offenders no matter how stable their emotional makeup.[46] This approach attempts to make offenders more competent members of the community (say, through useful employment) and, by improving societal acceptance of ex-offenders, aims to "reintegrate" the criminal into society.[47]

Whatever the approach—individualized punishment, treatment, or reintegration—rehabilitationists argue that the law should provide for differential handling of offenders based on their personal characteristics (rather than the offense) in order to increase the chances that they will subsequently choose to obey the law. The pervasiveness of the rehabilitative rationale and the persistence of competition among its various approaches are demonstrated in the commonly held belief that some criminals need to be taught a lesson (punishment), others need understanding (treatment), and others a socially approved job (reintegration) as assurance that they will stay out of trouble.

Notwithstanding its popularity as the primary justification of community supervision, there is a widespread perception that the rehabilitative ideal has failed. Although some empirical evidence has recently claimed a generally improved success rate for those placed on probation (compared with those incarcerated)[48] and those released on parole (compared with mandatory releases),[49] the landmark findings of Lipton, Martinson, and Wilks,[50] based on a survey of evaluative findings of over 200 correctional-treatment programs, have prompted a critical reevaluation of the utility of the rehabilitative model for correctional programming. In fact their conclusions do not differ much from those of other researchers who have summarized the effectiveness of treatment,[51] and they do not support a wholesale rejection of rehabilitative purposes, particularly in community supervision. For example, research has clearly called into question the legitimacy of the so-called medical model, which sometimes makes untenable assumptions about the etiology of a criminal's lawbreaking behavior.[52] On the other hand, recent direct-service models involving financial and employment services show early mixed results but offer some cause for optimism.[53] Evaluations of approaches that focus on specific offender behaviors and on contingencies related to those behaviors have been even more positive.[54] Likewise, it is now reasonably clear that uniform-treatment programs coercively applied, shotgun style, to a population of offenders are, "at best, wasteful": the programs have "helped some, hurt some, and had no effect on others."[55]

The interaction effect observed between type of treatment and type of client suggests that to be successful, rehabilitative programs need to put *more* emphasis on differential responses to offenders.[56] Most findings also question the success of *prison*-based rehabilitation. Whether the emphasis is on increased prison treatment or increased prison punishment, the evidence suggests little long-term success among offenders after their release.[57]

Similarly, research suggests that an emphasis on the traditionally preferred social-casework approach is not conceptually sound for all community-supervision offenders, particularly for adults. For juveniles, who may be more likely to accept the power differential in the relationship, "there is limited evidence that very small caseloads have proven to be effective."[58] The infusion of the social-work model into community supervision has been characterized

> by a failure to absorb two of the most basic tenets of social work. The first of these is that . . . the individual must perceive that he has a problem and be motivated to seek help. . . . The second is that the goals of the casework process must be established by the client.[59]

The potential usefulness of the rehabilitative model in community supervision probably lies in greater experimentation with direct service and with specialized interventions to alter the behavior of specific groups of offenders for whom some intervention has already proved effective.

Determining the Purpose of Community Supervision

It is clear from the discussion so far that the imposition of punishment—and community supervision as one mechanism of it—can serve a variety of purposes. Likewise, it is clear that rearranging the methods and tasks of those involved in the supervision process can create a shift in the emphasis of community supervision, depending on the aims being sought. The problem is that community supervision in the United States today is characterized by conflicting behaviors that make its purpose ambiguous and vitiate its effectiveness. The choice is not simply one between utilitarian (crime-control) and nonutilitarian (fairness-and-equity) values. The issue is how and to what degree to pursue utilitarian aims without violating nonutilitarian principles.

In scholarly circles, there appears to be growing support for non-utilitarian approaches to punishment. The prevailing opinion seems to be that because rehabilitation is a flawed philosophy, punishment ought to be determined solely on the basis of the seriousness of the offense. In this view, community supervision has little legitimacy, for it is normally imposed on the basis of offender characteristics (such as treatability) rather than offense characteristics and thus becomes a source of unwarranted disparity in punishment. The general public, in contrast, appears to be willing to adopt increasingly harsh approaches, if the new penal codes of Maine and Indiana are any indication. Although it is difficult to ascribe any value orientation to much of this legislation,[60] all of it appears to support generally harsher punishments, especially deterrence, desert, and incapacitation. From this perspective, community supervision is unacceptable simply because it is too lenient.

Both approaches emphasize incarcerative penalties at the expense of community-supervision penalties (which are, ironically, the most frequently given sentences). The erroneous belief that community supervision is something other than punishment needs to be rectified, and the design of any system of sanctions should include the option of keeping the offender in the community. A constrained risk-control approach addresses these dual purposes.

Constrained Risk Control

The Role of Retribution

The common belief is that retribution establishes a specific level of punishment that applies to each offense. Were this the case, determining that level would be difficult, for the seriousness of offenses with the same name varies. A battery resulting in temporary injury differs from one resulting in permanent disfiguration; a professional burglary involving irreplaceable artwork usually is considered more serious than a garage break-in involving tools.

In addition to these aggravating or mitigating factors, the offender's characteristics are often a consideration. Although most retributionists are loath to take into account the offender's age, risk, or socioeconomic status (the rejection of these factors is a prime basis for retributive logic), most are willing to change penalties to reflect the offender's previous record, on the grounds that a repeated offense is a more serious violation of social norms that a first one.[61]

In attempting to provide predictable and uniform sentences for similiar offenses strict retributionists usually array penalties along three dimensions—the offense, aggravating or mitigating factors, and previous record. The Twentieth Century Fund Task Force has acknowledged the complexity of this task by devoting an entire chapter to the problems of establishing penalties for one aspect of an assault law.[62] Given that many states' criminal codes list up to 1,000 unique offenses, the difficultly of establishing fixed, commensurate penalties for an entire penal code is appreciable.

Moreover, determining only the level of penalty that is deserved without taking other factors into account is exceedingly difficult. The commonest approach is to link retributive and deterrence concerns when deciding a punishment. For example, in establishing commensurate desert, von Hirsch argued that when seeking to justify the criminal sanction by reference to its deterrent effect, desert is called for to explain why that utility may be pursued at the offender's expense. When seeking to justify punishment as deserved, deterrence is needed to deal with the contravailing concern about suffering inflicted. The interdependence of these two concepts suggests that the criminal sanction rests, ultimately, on both.[63]

In fact the punitive and deterrent goals of punishment, though conceptually discrete, are in operation largely indistinguishable. Thus, the statement by the American Law Institute that punishments should not "depreciate the seriousness of the offense" expresses concern with both a social message (or threat) and a deserved punishment.[64]

How, then, can the legitimate values of desert reasonably be incorporated in a system of sanctions that also provides for risk control? In outlining a constrained risk-control approach in a community-supervision setting together with the methodologies required for implementation, we acknowledge that the principle of commensurate desert is of great importance to sentencing in a democratic society, not only because it is founded on a fundamental principle of justice that those who commit a crime deserve to be punished, but also because it holds that any particular offense deserves no more than an appropriate degree of punishment. Thus, desert asserts the fundamental principle of *proportionality,* namely, that a person should be punished according to the severity of the offense committed—no less and no more.

This principle has, with a few exceptions, been the dominant influence in American sentencing practices for a long time. Table 2-1, for example, shows the amount of time served in prison by a national sample of more than 100,000 offenders in the United States released during the period 1965-1970. The terms served reflect a variety of sentencing systems. Some featured high degrees of indeterminacy; that is, they permitted parole authorities to hold offenders for inordinate periods if they chose to do so. But despite these differences, it is clear that offenders in almost every jurisdiction served sentences closely linked to the severity of the crime committed. To this degree, the principle of commensurate desert has prevailed in the actual operation of sentencing systems in the United States.

However, table 2-1 also indicates that although there is a consistent relationship between time served and offense severity, there is considerable variation within offense categories in the amount of time served. This variation was one of the major bases for attacks on the indeterminate sentence, on the grounds that the basic principle of *equity*—that similarly situated offenders should be similarly treated—was being violated. To remedy this apparent injustice, it was argued, the discretion of parole boards and judges should be reduced or eliminated and a more predictable system adopted relating the precise amount of time served and the nature of the offense

Table 2-1
Median Time Served for Various Offenses by Mid-60
Percent in Each Category
(*months*)

Offense	Median Time Served	Range
Homicide	58.6	23-121
Forcible rape	49.5	20-106
Armed robbery	33.1	17-62
Other sex offenses	25.4	12-47
Unarmed robbery	24.8	13-43
Statutory rape	22.6	11-51
Manslaughter	20.8	11-42
Narcotics offenses	19.9	10-40
Burglary	16.2	9-29
Aggravated assault	15.4	7-30
Check fraud	14.7	9-24
Vehicle theft	13.8	8-23
Other theft, larceny	12.8	8-22
Other fraud	12.2	8-21

Source: Adapted from Don M. Gottfredson et al., *Four Thousand Lifetimes: A Study of Time Served and Parole Outcomes* (Davis, Calif.: National Council on Crime and Delinquency Research Center, 1973).

committed. As a result, in the past five years there has been a dramatic growth in the use of determinate sentencing in the United States. We agree that the type of crime should play a prominent role in determining punishment, but we disagree with the logic of determinate sentencing.

There is little argument among contemporary writers that the type of offense should fix the *range* of possible penalties. But using desert as a rationale for fixing a *precise* penalty in each individual case is a different matter. First, the tremendous variation in behavior within any given offense category makes it untenable to use only the type of crime committed to determine the exact sentence. The extensive attention paid by most determinate-sentencing schemes to aggravating and mitigating factors illustrates this problem. Second, it is impossible to impose a similar punishment on various individuals by simply making those who commit the same offenses serve precisely the same terms. There are great variations among types of prisons and programs, and there is even more variety in the responses of offenders to those environments. The variety in the deprivations imposed by the incarcerative environments and in the personal characteristics of offenders may make three months in jail more painful for one person than a year in prison for another. More important, affixing punishment solely on the basis of the type of crime is inevitably arbitrary, for desert-based schemes allow for no recourse to independent means of validation; it cannot be proved that a given sentence was appropriate or not. The decision rests on the judgment of those socially powerful enough to impose their views. The experience of jurisdictions that use a system of fixed or mandatory terms—the commonest means of operationalizing a desert-based system—has frequently been a significant and costly increase in the number of offenders incarcerated.

The Role of Risk Control

Perhaps most important, using desert as a basis for setting a specific sentence fails to respond to a result that virtually all citizens seek from a sentencing system, namely, crime control. The overriding desire of citizens who wish to be secure in their persons and property is the reduction and prevention of crime, not simply appropriate punishment. By definition, desert is not concerned with crime control. Its irrelevance to the almost uniform public desire for greater crime control may be a major reason why no contemporary sentencing reform has adopted the entire commensurate-desert approach, even though the values attached to it have often received legislative lip service.

The advocates of desert do, however, propose the use of an offender's previous criminal record as a consideration in fixing a sentence. Because that record is positively related to an offender's potential for recidivism, this provision also—whether deliberately or unintentionally—serves the ends of crime control and creates ambiguity in the standards used to determine a penalty. The great danger in this ambiguity—justice for some, crime control for others—is that it obscures goals and provides opportunities for inordinate punishment. Masking the pursuit of crime control under the label of desert enables authorities to justify draconian punishments that have no empirically demonstrable crime-control value simply on the grounds that they are "deserved."

This approach also deprives authorities of the kind of information most helpful for achieving crime control. In desert-oriented punishment schemes, information secured after sentencing is deemed irrelevant in determining the length of a term to be served by an offender. In contrast, crime-control orientation involves a high degree of interest in information about the offender that is developed after the time of sentencing.

Writers advocating a desert-based sentencing system have struggled, not too successfully, to resolve these problems.[65] One indication of this lack of clarity is found in the system used by the Oregon Parole Board to determine the length of sentence for an inmate. The matrix shown in Table 2-2 has been widely heralded as one that emphasizes proportionality of punishment rather than prediction of risk in fixing the prison term of an inmate. Closer examination, however, raises serious questions about this characterization.

Table 2-2
Oregon's Sentencing/Parole Matrix

| | Criminal-History/Risk-Assessment Score: Length of Sentence | | | |
Offense-Severity Rating	11-9 Excellent	8-6 Good	5-3 Fair	2-0 Poor
Category 1	−6	−6	6-12	12-22
Category 2	−6	6-10	10-18	18-28
Category 3	6-10	10-16	16-24	24-36
Category 4	10-16	16-22	22-30	30-48
Category 5	18-24	24-30	30-48	48-72
Category 6	36-48	48-60	60-86	86-144
Category 7				
subcategory 1	10-14 yrs.	14-19 yrs.	19-24 yrs.	24 yrs.-life
subcategory 2	8-10 yrs.	10-13 yrs	13-16 yrs.	16-20 yrs.

Note: Ranges in categories 1-6 are in months.

The matrix is indeed an outstanding example of a means of structuring discretion and a model for regularizing parole decision making. But it also reflects the type of compromise that characterizes most comtemporary sentencing-and parole-reform measures in the United States. The lefthand column of the matrix classifies offenses by seriousness, and the horizontal row presents the range of risk posed by the offender, scored by a predetermined scheme. It is quite clear that the lefthand column is essentially a desert statement, while the inmate's prior record and risk determine the horizontal values. It is also obvious that the enormous range in prison terms is dependent on prediction of individual's risk despite some obscuring of this point by an emphasis on the offender's prior record and the desert purpose this implies. Thus an offender convicted of perjury under Oregon law would be placed in category 2 and could serve from less than six up to twenty-eight months in prison, largely on the basis of assessed risk. Similarly, an offender convicted of an assault in the second degree (category 4) could serve from as little as ten months up to as much as four years, again based largely on the risk assessment. Comparison of these spans of time with those shown in table 2-1 raises the question whether there has in fact been a reduction of disparity—in strict desert terms—except for the most extreme cases.

Despite the fact that matrices of this kind place considerable emphasis on risk control and that the length of an offender's prison term is significantly determined by his assigned level of risk—indeed, in some cases more so than by the seriousness of the offense—we strongly favor their use. It is our position that risk control—the reduction of the probability of crime—should become an explicit purpose of sentencing. The upper and lower limits of appropriate punishment for a particular crime should be fixed by the notion of desert; within those limits, the purpose of a punishment should be risk control. Of course, one of the challenges in using risk control as a major dimension in determining the appropriate sentence for an individual is to minimize disparity of punishment—to limit the exercise of discretion in sentencing so that offenders at the same levels of risk are treated the same. The type of sentencing approach we advocate incorporates a mix of the traditional sentencing purposes. Experience has generally proved it to be sound and, with some modification capable of serving contemporary needs. We recommend that, within the limits established by the legislature, judges fix offenders' terms by using a matrix of the type shown in table 2-2.

This system would require sentences within the range shown for offense's seriousness rating (for example, ten to forty-eight months for category 4). This represents the upper and lower limits of deserved punishment. Within those limits, the risk posed by the offender would determine the precise length of sentence. Thus, an offender in category 4 who was very likely to commit further crimes would receive a sentence in the higher end of the range. Precise sentences would be fixed unambiguously on the basis of an assessment of risk. The consequences and assumptions of risk-related decisions would be stated openly and subject to test of their relative accuracy and appropriateness.

An objective means of risk assessment would be employed so that similar offenders are treated similarly, and so that dissimilar outcomes are justified on the basis of appropriate, risk-related criteria. The scale developed by the Oregon authorities for the risk dimension shown in table 2-2 is an example of one such objective measure, although variations have been developed for other jurisdictions. We expect that further experimentation would improve on existing models for sentencing.

A deserved punishment involves more than simply the length of a sentence, it also involves the circumstances under which that sentence is served. Thus broadly defined types of correctional settings (for example, institutions, community-based facilities, and community-supervision programs) must be linked with various levels of crime seriousness. For example, all offenders convicted of a type-1 offense might expect to be assigned, at least initially, to an institution, while all those convicted of a type-6 offense might expect to be assigned to community supervision. Because all punishment schemes must allow for some flexibility when attaching specific sanctions to specific offenders, we recognize the need for judicial discretion in selecting punishments. When a judge places an offender in a correctional setting other than that prescribed, a written explanation of the decision is required.

Once the initial term and correctional setting has been established by a judge, correctional authorities properly focus on two issues. The first issue is the risk posed by the convicted person. The second is the method of control needed to deal with that risk, including maximum-security prisons, minimum-security facilities, half-way houses, intensive supervision, or normal community supervision.

In order to structure a system of decision making that is fair and systematic, a series of explicit rules for assessing risk and determining control strategies must be developed. In the next chapter, we outline the features of such a set of rules, but it is important first to articulate some principles that would undergird any such rules.

Managing a Constrained Risk-Control System

Our fundamental aim is to develop a fair system of community protection in which incapacitative and treatment measures designed to control risk are employed rationally. It is a system constrained by the notion of desert, which fixes the range of acceptable punishment and encourages the use of such devices as restitution and community service.

Community protection is a complicated task, however, often involving trade-offs of benefits, cost determinations, and interaction effects with offenders.[66] Correctional managers may not take actions that jeopardize the safety of the community, but their decisions are not simple, for the best method to protect the public is not always clear. Moreover, two or more measures may carry roughly equivalent levels of risk control (such as community supervision and work release) and choices must be made among them.

Inevitably a considerable amount of discretion will remain with correctional managers, just as certain societal values constrain the way in which they manage the coercive power of the state when applied to the human beings in their charge. We believe that three important values—humaneness, knowledge utilization, and cost—have particular implications for the management of offenders.

Humaneness

As a management value, humaneness asserts both affirmative and negative guidance on correctional decision making. Negatively, the concern for humaneness means that interventions into offenders' lives must be limited to the least intrusive necessary to achieve the legitimate purposes of the criminal sanction. A criminal sentence is not a blank check for correctional administrators to implement favorite or convenient controls upon offenders. Humaneness limits discretion particularly with regard to treatment and incapacitative interventions and constantly tests decisions against potential alternative methods that are less intrusive.

Humaneness also requires that, wherever possible, the correctional administrator take actions that improve the life and potential of the offender while he or she is under the control of the state. The punishment involved in a criminal sentence is established through restrictions on the behaviors incurred as part of the sentence. Punishment cannot be augmented by refusal to provide basic services such as medical, educational, or vocational programs.

Knowledge

The management value of knowledge requires that those who make decisions regarding correctional measures recognize that risk control is a complicated concern. At a minimum, decisions must reflect an understanding of the effects of various options, familiarity with recent knowledge about corrections, and an ability to implement appropriate changes to improve effectiveness. Too frequently, correctional managers spend precious resources of time, money, and community credibility implementing new programs that, when attempted and evaluated in other settings, were only marginally effective. A concern for the management of knowledge requires building on what is known regarding effectiveness (as tentative as this knowledge may be) rather than compounding ineffective methods.

Moreover, the value of knowledge requires that correctional actions be undertaken in a way to improve our understanding of the impact of correctional policies. Evidence of limited effectiveness of commonly accepted approaches, a theme in all levels of criminal justice, requires that managers develop means to study the impact of all policy decisions, especially utilitarian programs of punishment.

Cost

Simply stated, cost values require that correctional managers adopt strategies that are least expensive to the state, other things being equal. Cost values alone do not justify the denial of desirable programs to offenders (this violates the principle of humaneness) or failure to protect the community or evaluate a new program. Thus, cost values are less important than the others.

There is also a tendency to adopt too narrow an interpretation of cost, using dollars as the only measure. A sufficiently broad definition takes into account potential costs in public credibility, the unknown costs of failing to attempt new approaches that might improve both effectiveness and efficiency, and the human costs involved in overextending state control over offenders' lives. Difficult as it may be to quantify these considerations, it is important not to underestimate them when attempting to keep costs to a minimum.

These values of humaneness, knowledge, and cost together justify a heavy reliance on community supervision as a primary form of the punitive sanction in criminal law. Notwithstanding the claims of much recent rhetoric, the effectiveness of imprisonment remains unclear at best. Although sophisticated statistical models have estimated that imprisonment has some deterrent effect,[67] other research finds no significant relation between incarceration rates and reported crime rates.[68] Despite some projections of the potential incapacitative benefits of imprisonment,[69] when applied to offender cohorts such models have demonstrated only a small potential effect on actual crime rates.[70] Both specific deterrence and rehabilitative rationales[71] fail to support incarcerative penalties.[72] Although recent research has questioned the degree of cost savings in programs designed to maximize the use of community supervision,[73] it is fair to say that traditional community programs are substantially cheaper than institutional alternatives, and evidence is growing that such options can be exercised without significant increases in risk to the community.[74]

In short, management values support continued reliance on community supervision approaches to risk control, absent conduct that deserves a greater restriction on liberty or evidence that community safety can be secured only through institutionalization.

Summary

In this chapter we have clarified the purposes of community supervision by showing how it may operate in ways relevant to each of the major approaches to punishing offenders. In arguing that the central purpose of community supervision is risk control, we have shown that risk-control aims are constrained by the nature and seriousness of the offense, normally thought of as commensurate desert and by certain societal values.

The following chapter describes how to make risk-control values operational in a community-supervision agency.

Notes

1. James D. Thompson, *Organizations in Action* (Englewood Cliffs, N.J.: Prentice-Hall, 1967).

2. Peter C. Drucker, *Management: Tasks—Responsibilities—Practices* (New York: Harper and Row, 1974).

3. Herman Goldstein, *Policing a Free Society* (Cambridge, Mass.: Ballinger, 1977).

4. For contrasting views see, for example, James Q. Wilson, *Thinking about Crime* (New York: Basic Books, 1975); and Twentieth Century Fund Task Force on Criminal Sentencing, *Fair and Certain Punishment* (New York: McGraw-Hill, 1976).

5. Andrew von Hirsch and Kathleen J. Hanrahan, *The Question of Parole: Retention, Reform, or Abolition?* (Cambridge, Mass.: Ballinger, 1979).

6. David Fogel, *". . . We Are the Living Proof . . .": The Justice Model for Corrections* (Cincinnati: Anderson, 1975).

7. Nicholas Kittrie, *The Right to Be Different* (Baltimore: Penguin, 1973).

8. See, for example, Reed K. Clegg, *Probation and Parole: Principles and Practices* (Springfield, Ill.: Charles C. Thomas, 1964); and David Dressler, *Practice and Theory of Probation and Parole* (New York: Columbia University Press, 1969).

9. See Alexander B. Smith and Louis Berlin, *Introduction to Probation and Parole* (St. Paul: West, 1976).

10. Naomi I. Brill, *Working with People: The Helping Process* (Philadelphia: Lippincott, 1973).

11. Dale G. Hardman, "Authority in Casework—a Bread and Butter Theory," in *Authority and Social Casework*, ed. Shankar A. Yelaja (Toronto: University of Toronto Press, 1971), p. 99.

12. Shankar A. Yelaja, "The Concept of Authority and Its Use in Child-Protective Services," in *Authority and Social Casework*, p. 234.

13. Paul W. Keve, *Imaginative Programming in Probation and Parole* (Minneapolis: University of Minnesota Press, 1967), p. 26.

14. Todd R. Clear, "Specification of Behavioral Objectives in Probation Supervision" (Ph.D. diss., State University of New York, 1977), p. 114.

15. Yelaja, "The Concept of Authority," p. 99.

16. Ernest van den Haag, *Punishing Criminals: On an Old and Painful Question* (New York: Basic Books, 1975), p. 25.

17. John Rawls, *A Theory of Justice* (Cambridge, Mass.: Harvard University Press, Belknap Press, 1971), p. 314.

18. van den Haag, *Punishing Criminals*, p. 15.

19. Nigel Walker, *The Aims of the Penal System* (Edinburgh: Edinburgh University Press, 1966), p. 67. For more detail on this view, see Andrew von Hirsch, *Doing Justice: The Choice of Punishments* (New York: Hill and Wang, 1976).

20. See Hyman Gross and Andrew von Hirsch, eds., *Sentencing* (New York: Oxford University Press, 1981).

21. Richard A. Salomon, "Lessons from the Swedish Criminal Justice System: A Reappraisal," *Federal Probation* 40, no. 3 (1976):40.

22. Arthur Rosset and Donald R. Cressey, *Justice by Consent* (Philadelphia: Lippincott, 1976).

23. U.S. Department of Justice, *State and Local Probation Systems* (Washington, D.C., 1978).

24. See, for example, Fogel, *We Are the Living Proof*, and von Hirsch, *Doing Justice*.

25. Stanley L. Benn and Richard S. Peters, *Social Principles and the Democratic State* (New York: Macmillan, 1959).

26. Herbert Packer, *The Limits of the Criminal Sanction* (Stanford, Calif.: Stanford Univ. Press, 1968), p. 24.

27. van den Haag, *Punishing Criminals*, p. 113.

28. Gordon Hawkins, "Punishment and Deterrence: The Educative, Moralizing, and Habituative Effects," *Wisconsin Law Review* 20 (1969): 530.

29. Johannes Andenaes, "The General Preventive Effects of Punishment," *University of Pennsylvania Law Review* 114 (1966):955.

30. Jack Gibbs, "Crime, Punishment, and Deterrence," *Southwestern Social Science Quarterly* 48, no. 1 (1968):51.

31. Gordon Tullock, "Does Punishment Deter Crime?" *Public Interest* 36 (1975):103.

32. Ibid.

33. See, for example, National Council on Crime and Delinquency, *Model Sentencing Act* (New York, 1963); compare with *Indiana Criminal Law and Procedure* (St. Paul: West, 1978), sec. 35.

34. Marc Ancel, *Social Defense: A Modern Approach to Criminal Problems* (London: Schocken Books, 1965), p. 13.

35. Norval Morris and Gordon Hawkins, *An Honest Politician's Guide to Crime Control* (Chicago: University of Chicago Press, 1970), p. 68.

36. Wilson, *Thinking about Crime*, p. 173.

37. Ibid.; see also Marvin E. Wolfgang, "Crime in a Birth Cohort," *Proceedings of the American Philosophical Society* 117 (1973):404.

38. Andrew von Hirsch, *Doing Justice*, p. 4.

39. van den Haag, *Punishing Criminals*, p. 244.

40. Federal Judicial Center, "Probation Time Study," mimeographed (Washington, D.C., 1973).

41. David T. Stanley, *Prisoners among Us: The Problem of Parole* (Washington, D.C.: Brookings Institution, 1976), p. 126.

42. Ibid., p. 101.

43. See, for example, People v. Dominguez, 256 Cal. App. 623 (1967); Matter of Hernandez, no. 76757 at 12 (Calif. Sup. Ct. 1966); and Hyland v. Procunier, 311 F. Supp. 749 (1970).

44. Robert M. Carter, Richard A. McGee, and E. Kim Nelson, *Corrections in America* (Philadelphia: Lippincott, 1975), p. 5.

45. Edwin M. Schur, *Radical Non-Intervention: Rethinking the Delinquency Problem* (Englewood Cliffs, N.J.: Prentice-Hall, 1973), p. 31.

46. See Richard A. Cloward and Lloyd E. Ohlin, *Delinquency and Opportunity: A Theory of Delinquent Gangs* (New York: Free Press, 1960).

47. President's Commission on Law Enforcement and the Administration of Justice, *The Challenge of Crime in a Free Society* (Washington, D.C.: Government Printing Office, 1967).

48. Ted Bartell and L. Thomas Winfree, "Recidivist Impacts of Differential Sentencing Practices for Burglary Offenders," *Criminology* 15 (1977):387.

49. See William H. Moseley, "Parole: How Is It Working?" *Journal of Criminal Justice* 5, no. 3 (1977):185; and Robert Martinson and Judith Wilks, "Save Parole Supervision," *Federal Probation* 41, no. 3 (1977):23.

50. Douglas Lipton, Robert Martinson, and Judith Wilks, *The Effectiveness of Correctional Treatment* (New York: Praeger, 1975).

51. See Leslie T. Wilkins, *Evaluation of Penal Measures* (New York: Random House, 1969); James Robison and Gerald Smith, "The Effectiveness of Correctional Programs," *Crime and Delinquency* 17 (1971):67; and Walter C. Bailey, "Correctional Treatment: An Analysis of One Hundred Outcome Studies," *Journal of Criminal Law, Criminology, and Police Science* 62, no. 3 (1966):153.

52. See, for example, Gene Kassebaum, David Ward, and Ed Wilner, *Prison Treatment and Parole Survival: An Empirical Assessment* (New York: Wiley, 1971).

53. Kenneth Lenihan, "Financial Aid for Released Prisoners: An Experiment in Reducing Recidivism" (Paper presented at the meeting of the American Society of Criminology, Atlanta, November 1977); Robert Evans, "The Labor Market and Parole Success," *Journal of Human Resources* 3 (1968):207; and "An Analysis of the Federal Bonding Program," mimeographed (Contract Research Corporation, Belmont, Mass., 1975).

54. Bob Ross and Paul Gendreau, *Effective Corrections* (Toronto: Butterworks, 1980).

55. Marguerite Q. Warren, "All Things Being Equal . . . ," *Criminal Law Bulletin* 9 (1973):483, 484; see also Ted Palmer, "Martinson Revisited," *Journal of Research in Crime and Delinquency* 12 (1975):230.

56. Stuart Adams, "Effectiveness of Interview Therapy with Older Youth Authority Wards: An Interim Evaluation of the PICO Project Research Report no. 20," mimeographed (California Youth Authority, Sacramento, 1961).

57. Don M. Gottfredson, Michael R. Gottfredson, and James Garofalo, "Time Served in Prison and Parole Outcomes among Parolee Risk Categories," *Journal of Criminal Justice* 5, no. 1 (1977):1; and Kassebaum, Ward, and Wilner, *Prison Treatment and Parole Survival.*

58. James Banks, et al., *Phase I Evaluation of Intensive Special Probation Projects* (Washington, D.C.: U.S. Department of Justice, 1977), p. 5.

59. National Advisory Commission on Criminal Justice Standards and Goals, *Corrections* (Washington, D.C.: Government Printing Office, 1973), p. 16.

60. For discussion of the Maine penal code, see M.G. Neithercutt, "Parole Legislation," *Federal Probation* 41, no. 1 (1977):22. For discussion of the Indiana penal code, see Todd R. Clear, John D. Hewitt, and Robert M. Regoli, "Discretion and the Determinate Sentence: Its Distributions, Control, and Effect on Time Served," *Crime and Delinquency* 24 (1978):428.

61. See von Hirsch, *Doing Justice.*

62. Twentieth Century Fund Task Force, *Fair and Certain Punishment*

63. von Hirsch, *Doing Justice*, p. 34.

64. American Law Institute, *Model Penal Code: Proposed Official Draft* (Philadelphia, 1962).

65. Andrew von Hirsch, "Desert and Previous Convictions in Sentencing," *Minnesota Law Review* 65 (April 1981).

66. For an example of the policy-related debate on benefit tradeoffs, see Marlene W. Lehniten, "The Value of Life—an Argument for the Death Penalty;" and Gerald W. Smith, "The Value of Life—Arguments against the Death Penalty," both in *Crime and Delinquency* 23 (1977):237 and 253, respectively. For the second and third considerations, see, respectively, Neil M. Singer, "Economic Implications of Standards for Correctional Institutions," *Crime and Delinquency* 23 (1977):14; and Warren, "All Things Being Equal," p. 483.

67. Tullock, "Does Punishment Deter Crime?" p. 103.

68. William G. Nagel, "On Behalf of a Moratorium on Prison Construction," *Crime and Delinquency* 23 (1977):154.

69. See Wilson, *Thinking about Crime.*

70. Stephen Van Dine, Simon Dinitz, and John Conrad, "The Incapacitation of the Dangerous Offender: A Statistical Study," *Journal of Research in Crime and Delinquency* 14 (1977):22.

71. Don M. Gottfredson et al., *Four Thousand Lifetimes: A Study of Time Served and Parole Outcomes* (Davis, Calif.: National Council on Crime and Delinquency Research Center, 1973).

72. Lipton, Martinson, and Wilks, *The Effectiveness of Correctional Treatment.*

73. Paul Lerman, *Community Treatment and Social Control* (Chicago: University of Chicago Press, 1975).

74. A series of evaluations of the community supervision in Wisconsin support its effectiveness. See especially S. Christopher Baird, et al., *The Wisconsin Workload Classification Project—Two Year Follow Up* (Washington, D.C.: National Institute of Corrections, 1982).

3 Some Principles for Implementing Risk Control

Historically, three important difficulties with risk control have led many to question its appropriateness in a system of state sanctions; prediction error, abuse of discretion, and lack of valid risk-prediction techniques. Among the most troublesome kinds of prediction errors are those that lead to unnecessarily intrusive correctional interventions. Other abuses of discretion may occur as a result of the fallibility of decision makers or because reliable and valid information has not been systematically identified and made readily available to them. Under these conditions, the exercise of discretion can result in arbitrary or capricious judgments about offenders. However, some authorities believe that measures taken to guard against personal or systematic failings cannot be effective because ultimately no valid risk-prediction technology now exists. If a system of sanctions based on risk control is to meet the test of fairness, ways must be found to deal with these problems. In this chapter we describe means to increase the reliability of risk-control measures and to control the exercise of discretion.

Prediction Errors

Any model of corrections based on risk control must use some form of prediction, and any prediction approach will make some errors, simply because it is impossible to specify in advance an offender's precise future behavior. Later in this chapter, we describe technologies that increase the accuracy of predictions; first, however, we must address the ethical problem created by the existence of prediction errors.

Two types of error are possible in the prediction of risk. False negatives are the most visible: a person predicted to be "safe" (that is, a negative risk), and consequently placed under reduced restraint commits a serious crime. Much of the current concern about punishment is based on a desire to minimize this kind of error because it results in victims of crime.[1] Another type of error, false positives (overpredictions), is less visible: an offender predicted to be a risk is kept under close control, even though he or she would not have committed a crime under less severe restraints. Some recent writers, in criticizing the unfairness of a system that results in false positives—an offender is restrained because of what others believe he or she might do, not because of what the offender has already done—have thereby concluded that all risk prediction is unethical.[2] One consequence of this type of concern about prediction error has been a general move toward mandatory, determinate sentences for all people convicted of serious offenses.[3]

Attempts to eliminate error by eliminating prediction, however, will ultimately fail, because risk-control aims cannot be separated from the practices of corrections and punishment. Risk control is an inevitable aspect of any modern sentencing system. A recent comment by Aryeh Neier of the American Civil Liberties Union illustrates the difficulty of keeping risk control concerns out of sentencing and correctional decisions. When asked whether parole should be abolished, Neier replied:

> Parole . . . assumes . . . authorities can predict future crimes on the basis of prison behavior. This is unfair to everyone. Predictions based on prison behavior have proved wholly unreliable. . . . Even for the most vicious crimes, a maximum sentence of 15 years—without parole—is adequate. . . . It would protect society since few crimes are committed by people after their mid-30s.[4]

Clearly, Neier's approach is predictive: it makes an assumption regarding the likelihood of future crime by offenders who have committed "vicious crimes" and have been incarcerated up to the age of thirty before being released. The difference is that this particular prediction ignores information other than an offender's crime and age and is the same for all offenders in certain offense and age categories—an approach that actually increases prediction errors. While claiming to reject the technology of prediction, Neier has made an implicit prediction, one hidden under a blanket policy. It is virtually impossible to eliminate concern for risk from criminal law, whether one represents a liberal perspective as Neier, or a more conservative one. Thus, in most current public proposals for mandatory sentences, stronger penalties for recidivists and abolition of parole reflect a much greater emphasis on risk prediction than on equity. The common shortcoming of almost all of these approaches is the blanket prediction they inherently assume about large classes of offenders.

These approaches suffer from at least two problems. First, by ignoring additional risk-relevant information and focusing only on the current (and perhaps prior) criminal behavior, they reject information that might lead to a more sophisticated predictive equation. Given that complex models already tend to overpredict risk, false positives are likely to increase with a simple across-the-board approach. The punishment imposed will have been more severe than necessary for achieving either risk control or justice.

Understandable and widespread concerns about protecting the public and getting offenders off the street are inevitably converted into sentencing laws heavily reflective of risk-control aims such as incapacitation. However, attempting to implement such aims through blanket policies that do not allow for predictions of an individual's risk under alternative dispositions has enormously unfair and costly results. Much attention has been given to the problem of the false positive—the person subjected to unwarranted state control because of an inaccurate prediction. But little concern has been expressed about another and *much larger group*—those who would be subjected to unnecessary state control if a system of individualized risk assessment were *not* employed.

Second, relying on models that use an offense as the only basis for unarticulated predictions guarantees low rates of success in reducing crime, and at a high cost. A recent study conducted by the Academy for Contemporary Problems concluded that a five-year mandatory prison term for all offenders convicted of violent offenses would have resulted in a net decrease in reported violent offenses of less than 2 percent at a substantial cost in overprediction and unnecessary incarceration.[5]

Notwithstanding the dissatisfaction with risk-predictive approaches, "reliance on prediction appears inevitable."[6] Attempts to eliminate risk prediction are likely to result in more abusive systems (as has been the case with most recent sentencing reforms), because punishment policy "is as much influenced by public mood and political consideration as it is by empirical evidence of crime causation and control."[7] The fact that so much of the current debate stems from a public concern about rising crime is sufficient to guarantee that reforms enacted in the political context will reflect concern for utilitarian goals such as risk control. However, the ways in which the new reforms are designed result in expensive and ineffective means of crime control that impose intrusive and costly penalties on the basis of faulty assumptions about risk and techniques of incapacitation.

If risk control aims are inevitable, reformers and decision makers must face the existence of error in a straightforward manner. Only then can the amount and nature of prediction error be made visible and controlled; only then can the amount of error be kept to a minimum through routinized prediction policy.

The greatest number of errors in prediction occur when the criterion is an infrequent behavioral event. Violent behavior, for example, has proved to be a sufficiently infrequent event, even for individuals exhibiting past violent behavior, that "neither statistical nor clinical prediction of dangerousness has been demonstrated."[8] The poor results in predicting extreme events have led some to conclude that "low base rates cannot be predicted sufficiently to warrant their use in clinical practice."[9] In a recent survey of violence-prediction studies, Monahan found that false-positive rates ranged from 54 percent to over 99 percent and concluded that

> violence is vastly overpredicted whether simple behavioral indicators are used or sophisticated multivariate analyses are employed, and whether psychological tests are administered or thorough psychiatric examinations are performed.[10]

It is clear that errors are much more likely to occur in attempts to predict a rare event such as murder than in predictions of a more common one such as burglary.[11]

Moreover, the relation between risk and the amount and type of error a decision maker might be willing to accept is not a simple one. For example, Wilkins has argued that the amount of overprediction that is acceptable should increase as the severity of the behavior predicted increases.[12] Conversely, as the degree of risk diminishes, the extent of overprediction, and hence unnecessary state control, that is acceptable should also decrease. This is an important principle for community supervision where the degree of intrusiveness into the lives of offenders is less extreme than it is for those who are serving their sentences in prison. A policy favoring community interventions can minimize the harsh results caused by overprediction in the use of incarcerative interventions and greatly reduce costs, with little or no additional risk to the public. Thus, we advocate a policy that acknowledges the possibility of error while rejecting the pretense

> that there is some magical way to run a correctional system without any risk. Every course of action involves risk. The choice is really between continuing to take the old risks . . . or to take some new ones . . . and rationalize the risk-taking process.[13]

We attempt to rationalize the risk-taking process and to exert more control over the type of error a predictive system produces.

To be just, any process based on prediction must meet several criteria: it must be based on a valid model of risk assessment; there must be a structure for decision making; the structure must produce a high degree of reliability in its application; and there must be flexibility built into the system. As a step toward refining these principles, we address the crucial problems of technology and structure for decision making.

Prediction Technology

The first task is to identify prediction methods that are relatively accurate. Reliance on a risk-control model assumes the use of information that identifies the offender as requiring, for some reason, increased control by correctional authorities. This increased control is "morally and legally legitimate only if we can accurately determine those persons to whom such special treatment should apply."[14]

A number of studies have shown that the fundamental task of devising a valid method for differentiating risk is a difficult one.[15] There are two basic approaches to prediction: actuarial (or statistical) and clinical (or judgmental). For each of these approaches, several variants are often used.

Clinical predictions are normally made by an individual after some form of case analysis. This has been typically defined as "the problem-solving or decision-making behavior of a person who tries to reach conclusions regarding risk on the basis of facts or theories already available to him by thinking them over."[16] One unfortunate consequence of using so broad a definition is that even the most incompetent guesswork by nonprofessionals comes to be seen as clinical prediction. Most trained clinicians see prediction as a complex process. In describing one clinical model, Cohen, Groth, and Siegal argue that it requires

> a minimum of a 60-day period . . . Sources for prediction are clinical interviews, psychological tests, official records and transcripts, family interviews, behavioral reports of the offender's adjustment during the observation period, field investigations, and, where relevant, interviews with the victim. Only after completing this process is a predictive decision made.[17]

This description probably applies more to an ideal process than to the actual manner in which most agencies undertake the tasks of prediction.

Actuarial or statistical predictions rely on less information than clinical approaches but tend to use the information in a more systematic way. Normally, building a statistical-prediction device involves several steps.

> In parole prediction the records of the prisoners paroled in past years are tabulated statistically to determine the violation rate for each group into which these past parolees could have been classified at release. Thus, separate violation rates are determined for each age, offense, prior criminal record, and other statistical categories. There are several methods of combining this information to get an overall prediction. One of the simplest procedures is to assign a "parole success score" to each past parolee by giving him one point for each item on which he is in a category which had less than average violation rates, and either none, or minus points, for items in which he is in a category with above average violation rates. For example, a prisoner might get one point for being above 40 years old, one point for having the offense of manslaughter, one point for being a first offender, and so forth. Violation rates, then, are determined for each score; thus parolees with 12 points may have had only a 10% violation rate, as compared with 40% for those with only five favorable points and 80% for those with no points.[18]

Statistical models, then, are similar to the tables that determine insurance premiums. Based on the subject's most salient characteristics, a probability score is calculated; the resulting percentage figure states the proportion of individuals possessing the same characteristics who have exhibited the criteria (such as violent offenses) in the past. Figure 3-1 shows a risk-screening instrument used in Ohio. This approach identifies variables associated with risk and arranges them in a screening device that enables a

Number of Prior Felony Convictions (or Juvenile Adjudications)	0	None
	2	One
	4	Two or more _____

| Arrested within Five (5) Years prior to Arrest for Current Offense (excludes traffic) | 0 | No |
| | 4 | Yes _____ |

Age at Arrest Leading to First Felony Conviction (or Juvenile Adjudications)	0	24 and over
	2	20-23
	4	19 and under _____

Amount of Time Employed in Last 12 Months (prior to Incarceration for Parolees)	0	More than 7 months
	1	5 to 7 months
	2	Less than 5 months
	0	Not applicable _____

Alcohol Usage Problems (prior to Incarceration for Parolees	0	No interference with functioning
	2	Occasional abuse; some disruption of functioning
	4	Frequent abuse; serious disruption; needs treatment _____

Other Drug Usage Problems (prior to Incarceration of Parolees)	0	No interference with functioning
	2	Occasional abuse; some disruption of functioning
	4	Frequent abuse; serious disruption; needs treatment _____

Number of Prior Adult Incarcerations in a State or Federal Institution	0	0
	3	1-2
	6	3 and above _____

Age at Admission to Institution or Probation for Current Offense	0	30 and over
	3	18-29
	6	17 and under _____

| Number of Prior Adult Probation/Parole Supervisions | 0 | None |
| | 4 | One or more _____ |

| Number of Prior Probation/Parole Revocations Resulting in Imprisonment (Adult or Juvenile) | 0 | None |
| | 4 | One or more _____ |

Total _____

Figure 3-1. Ohio's Risk-Screening Instrument

rater to estimate the risk potential of an offender by summing the weighted values of the variables; the higher the score, the greater the risk. Clinical methods, on the other hand, normally result in dichotomous predictions: the person either will or will not exhibit the targeted behavior; decision makers may also use clinical methods to array people into general risk groups.

Paul Meehl conducted one of the earliest and still most widely cited comparisons of statistical and clinical studies. Despite his acknowledgment that the prediction studies he reviewed were not "optimally designed to exhibit the clinician at his best," Meehl concluded that the preponderance of the evidence indicated the superiority of statistical methods.[19] Other researchers have been less hesitant in supporting statistical approaches, even early in their development. In 1943, for example, Sarbin argued that actuarial models should replace clinical models at virtually every stage of the diagnostic phases in hospitals and schools, making clinical evaluation "a secondary function."[20] Since Meehl's evaluation, numerous studies indicating the effectiveness of statistical models have been reported.[21] Lloyd Ohlin used a Burgess scale (a weighting scheme for calculating scores by assigning + 1 for each offender characteristic correlated to success and − 1 for each factor related to failure) to predict accurately the outcomes of 72 percent of 4,941 parole cases. Although Ohlin believed that "no single device which social scientists may contrive can adequately supplant parole board members,"[22] he felt that these scores could make the board "aware of the risks involved" so that "mistakes that occur will simply be errors of judgment, and will not be due to lack of information as to the potentiality of violation."[23] the United States Parole Commission continues to use a similar prediction device in making parole decisions.[24]

Mannheim and Wilkins used a more sophisticated factor-analysis design to predict training-school releasee behavior and found that "the statistical classification into likely failure and likely success groups results in more than twice the accuracy of intuitive methods based on judgments of highly experienced assessors."[25] In their view, "the two methods together are likely to result in better classification than any one alone."[26] In a recent study of the work-release success of Virginia parolees, discriminant-function analysis predicted correctly in over 70 percent of the cases, a significant improvement over the clinical predictions.[27] These results demonstrate why there is now greater willingness to rely on statistical models in decision making.

Statistical risk-prediction models have also proved useful for probation supervision. A recent report by the U.S. Comptroller General "tested the validity and predictive powers of [eight] existing models by applying them to 900 closed cases"[28] selected from three counties. Three of the models were found to be useful in identifying risk for the offenders. The report concluded that

> probation prediction models could improve probation systems operations by allocating resources to offenders who most need help. . . . Model sources appeared to be useful in determining supervision levels and more successfuly selected probationers for early release.[29]

These and other research efforts indicate that statistical methods are efficient means of identifying client risk. However, clinical prediction is not obsolete. A number of studies indicate that clinical-prediction methods have a great deal to offer and, under some circumstances, may even be superior to statistical models. One recent review of studies of clinical prediction concluded that

> the only two studies that could truly be called clinical-prediction . . . show considerable improvements over the statistical studies in both false positive and false negative error rates and demonstrate . . . that a conclusion about our capability of predicting dangerousness is premature.[30]

Studies that have attempted to correct methodological errors in much of the earlier research have also produced results confirming the potential value of clinical prediction.[31] Meehl, for example, in a follow-up study to his earlier work, found that pooled clinical judgments were not substantially less accurate than pooled statistical methods.[32] Robert Hold found that providing the clinician with a prediction structure is also helpful.

> When social workers rated an initial interview according to their general impressions, they were unable to predict the outcome of the case, whereas when their judgments were organized and guided by means of an outline calling for appraisal of five factors which had been shown in previous research to be *meaningfully,* not statistically related to the criterion, then these judgments derived predictive variables . . . predicted the criterion quite well.[33]

Moreover, Don Gottfredson has noted that statistical models cannot easily handle contingency-specific risk predictions: "Prediction tables appear static; they seem to assume no changes will occur in the personal or social conditions that might alter the prediction."[34] This is an important point to underscore, for decision makers are more concerned with predicting the effectiveness of various methods of control for various offenders than with simply predicting whether, in general, clients are likely to commit new offenses. For example, suppose an offender has exhibited a long pattern of assaultive behavior and is in a class of offenders in which 40 percent are likely to commit crimes again. Suppose further that it appears the offender has gotten into trouble only when drinking excessively. Two predictions beyond the general probability of recidivism become central: the likely precise relationship between the offender's behavior and drinking and the likelihood of controlling that drinking pattern.

Unfortunately, most studies of statistical predictions have been concerned only with whether given classes of offenders would succeed or fail. Very few have dealt with the type of contingencies suggested in our example. One reason is that it is very difficult to get reliable information about these kinds of relationships in the case records on which most research depends. Second, contingency estimates are impossible to calculate reliably without a large sample. And third, the tremendous variety and combinations possible make systematic predictions of this type exceedingly difficult to make in simple statistical terms. These pedictions must rely heavily on clinical judgments.

Such predictions are made and acted upon daily in correctional settings, where the ability to manage events through risk-control measures is greater than is the case with predictions of general recidivism. Moreover, to the extent that the risk level and type of error are known in such cases, the probability increases that decisions will be more accurate, more effective (in terms of minimizing error), and more reliable.

Thus it is clear that to present clinical and statistical prediction as alternatives is simplistic. Both approaches provide benefits. The optimal model will rest on both, enabling decision makers to use validated prediction scales as aids to making probablistic judgments.[35]

Structure for Decision Making

In general, the most-effective way to increase decision reliability is to make the criteria for decisions visible within a decision-making structure.[36] For that reason, we advocate the use of statistically based devices to classify offenders according to relative risk. It is also important to limit the criteria indicating risk to as few explicit items as possible, a characteristic of statistical predictions. When a number of people are responsible for making risk decisions, the use of a standard instrument, such as the Ohio one shown earlier, makes the assessment decision substantially more reliable—that is, various decision makers are more likely to reach the same conclusion. This does not mean that clinical judgments are unnecessary. They are crucial to an effectively operated system. However, when a clinical judgment leads to a risk classification different from the one suggested by a statistical device, an appropriate official should decide whether or not to accept that judgment. The decision to override the findings of the statistical device would have to depend on the reputation and experience of the person making the clinical assessment, the circumstances under which it was made, and the specific factors considered.

By definition, predictions require concrete prognostic statements about a person's future behavior. However, statements such as "Offender X will commit a new crime" are highly susceptible to error. In contrast, the risk-screening approach just described lends itself to statements of relative probability such as "Offender A is in a class of individuals not very likely to commit an offense, but more likely than the class of individuals in which offender B is located." The latter statement is more defensible from a risk-management point of view because it enables an agency to classify offenders systematically according to their *relative* risk. Table 3-1 illustrates such a risk-screening approach. As the score increases, so does the rearrest rate of prior offenders with that score. The aggregate scores show that offenders with a score of 0-10 have a reconviction rate of 9.3 percent, while offenders with a score of 21 and over have a reconviction rate of 65.6 percent. Instead of making predictions, this instrument in effect classifies offenders according to their relative potential for rearrest—or, more accurately, according to the risk potential indicated by their aggregate characteristics. In addition to clarifying the risk criteria, this approach also makes visible the amount and character of prediction error involved in various decisions. It becomes possible to say, for example, that about one-third of those classified as high risk (21 and over) will not commit offenses (false positives) and that less than one-tenth of those classified as low risk (0-10) will commit offenses (false negatives). Structuring the risk-assessment process makes it possible to know the nature and degree of error likely to exist. Thus, prediction becomes more manageable and more reliable as an aid to purposeful policy-making.[37] Policymakers can reduce the ratio of false positives to false negatives and improve knowledge about risk control.

Consistency in Risk Control

A given risk score does not automatically lead to fixed programmatic decisions. If a risk-control model is to operate fairly, however, there must be some programmatic consistency, especially since so little is known about which programs will be most effective in controlling risk. Consistency can-

Table 3-1
Rates of Reconviction for Various Risk-Assessment Scores

Risk-Assessment Score	Actual Rate of Reconviction	
	Percent	Number
0-5	6.3	48
6-10	10.2	177
11-15	28.9	201
16-20	46.4	166
21-25	63.2	76
26-31	76.5	17
Total	31.7	685

Source: Todd Clear and Ken Gallagher, "New Jersey Case Management Project" (Report to the National Institute of Corrections, (Washington, D.C., 1981).

Note: Rates reflect all types of violations and all arrests for a three-year followup period subsequent to supervision.

not depend on narrowly defined types of disposition such as "two years in prison." It requires a broader base of alternatives from which specific choices are made based on an assessment of an offender's circumstances. Moreover, the availability of given programs will vary from area to area, and the offender's willingness to participate will vary among persons of equivalent risk levels. Essentially, risk-control programs are structured around the *level* of security required for an offender. We recommend a procedure that would operate as follows.

First, the seriousness of the offense would determine not only the maximum term of the penalty but also the initial setting for correctional control (prison, jail, or probation). This criterion satisfies the elementary requirements of justice.

Second, the intrusiveness of programs would be ranked according to their degree of intervention in the life of the offender, as in the following scale:

Maximum Intrusiveness: Maximum-security prison
Medium-security prison
Minimum-security prison

Medium Intrusiveness: Local correctional facility
Halfway house
Intensive surveillance in community

Minimum Intrusiveness: Community supervision on probation or parole
Community service/restitution
Minimum probation supervision

The programs in each intrusiveness category provide a roughly equivalent amount of public protection. In medium-intrusiveness category, for example, the actual proportion of serious crimes committed by parolees while under supervision is relatively small, perhaps in the order of 10 to 15 percent of those released to supervision. Intensive surveillance in community supervision, as opposed to traditionally sized caseloads, can further reduce this low level of crime and provide the same order of public protection as incarceration in a local correctional facility or halfway house.

Third, a maximum limit would be placed on the amount of time a person may spend in a risk-control sanction of a given level of intrusiveness unless additional time can be justified through an appropriate review process. Table 3-2 illustrates how this approach might work. Thus, an offender convicted of a class-C offense might be limited to no more than, say, six months at the initial risk-control assignment, with the total time under control to be two years. A more-serious, class-A offender might be held in the initial risk-control level for a longer period.

Table 3-2
Illustration of Risk-Control Program Principles

Seriousness of Offense	Maximum Duration of Control	Original Risk-Control Assignment	Rate of Movement
A	6 years	maximum	2 years
B	4 years	maximum or medium	1 year
C	2 years	medium or minimum	6 months
D	1 year	minimum	3 months

Three important features undergird this system. First, the offender's risk determines the type of initial program assignment so long as it is consistent with the seriousness of the offense. Second, movement through the security levels is predictable. That is, the expected duration of assignment to an initial level of risk control would be preordained according to the severity of the offense. Third, movement beyond the initial reduction in control level is based on an assessment of risk. The result in the example is a system in which an offender convicted of a class-B offense would spend one year in maximum risk control and would progress through lesser controls, with the total duration of control not to exceed four years. While the scheduling of time and rate of movement might be open to debate, the consistency of a risk-control process depends on these three requirements.

The principle of humaneness also requires systematic provision of opportunities for offenders to demonstrate their ability to live without severe restrictions on their behavior. Moreover, it is the responsibility of corrections to design risk-management programs at every level of intrusion whose effect is to reduce the offender's risk to the community. Although not all offenders will benefit equally from programs, no program should be denied to an offender if there is a rational basis for providing it. At the same time, the fact that offenders may exhibit the same level of risk does not mean they will always be handled in the same way. For example, two offenders of, say, 20-percent risk might be handled differently in the initial assignment to programs of equivalent intrusiveness. One person might be assigned work release to deal with a problem of unemployment, and the other placed under intensive community supervision while dealing with an alcohol problem. These differences could also persist after the initial risk-control assignment. Thus, the nature of the offender's risk (beyond the raw level of risk) should help to determine the risk-control intervention used throughout the process.

The Need for System Flexibility

The elements discussed above are not the only ways to implement risk control while managing problems of discretion and error. Variations in sentence terms and in rates of movement are possible so long as they are not excessive. Individual offenders could move more quickly through intervention levels if decision makers so determine. Likewise, some offenders might move more slowly, particularly if their behavior clearly indicates that a given level of control does not ensure adequate public protection. The flexibility permitted to decision makers must be accompanied by procedures to protect offenders from infringements on due-process rights and by provision for administrative review.

Thus we envision a risk-control system that incorporates at a minimum the following features:

1. Use of standard assessment instruments that make decision criteria visible, testable, and subject to continuing research
2. Use of known groupings for risk classification that make the type and amount of prediction error visible
3. The establishment of limits on the nature and duration of interventions into offenders' lives, based on the seriousness of the offense
4. The placement of offenders into initial intervention programs on the basis of risk but commensurate with offense seriousness
5. The establishment of routine, consistent schedules for reducing the intrusiveness of the risk-control method
6. The establishment of decision-review mechanisms that prevent arbitrariness in initial assignments and in acceleration or retardation of an offender's movement through programs

Such an approach has several advantages over current methods. First, it minimizes error but also makes error visible so that it can be studied and further reduced. Second, it provides a mechanism for controlling the discretion of decision makers who apply risk-control criteria to offenders. Third, it establishes a routine practice for risk control that makes the corrections function more predictable.

Were this a book on sentencing, we would have to elaborate on this general model: What modifications are needed to deal with serious multiple recidivists? Is more flexibility needed for dealing with unusually heinous offenses? The nature of criminal behavior and offenders is sufficiently varied that the law would need to provide for a wide variety of circumstances. Yet the model we have described is applicable to the vast majority of offenders who must be routinely handled by corrections, and it demonstrates how reliability, predictability, and control of discretion can be built into risk control.

Summary

In this chapter we have described some principles for implementing a risk-control approach to corrections. The centerpiece of these principles is a structured approach to risk assessment based on standardized, statistical instruments. Programmatic decisions, such as initial program assignment and nature and rate of movement, have been included in a framework that makes them more predictable.

The purpose of these principles is to increase the reliability of risk-control decisions while making them more visible so that they can be systematically controlled and studied. Given that it is impossible to eliminate risk-control errors, the task of corrections is to minimize those errors and manage their distribution while implementing programs that promote humaneness.

In the chapters that follow, we describe the community-supervision function from the vantage point of these risk-control principles. Part II provides a detailed description of the operation of risk-control practices in supervision. Part III describes management applications of those practices.

Notes

1. Ernest van den Haag, *Punishing Criminals: On an Old and Painful Question* (New York: Basic Books, 1975); James Q. Wilson, *Thinking about Crime* (New York: Basic Books, 1975); see especially U.S. Department of Justice, *Attorney General's Task Force on Violent Crime* (Washington, D.C., 1981).

2. See, for example, Andrew von Hirsch, *Doing Justice: The Choice of Punishments* (New York: Hill and Wang, 1976); David Fogel, *". . . we are the living proof . . .": The Justice Model for Corrections* (Cincinnati: Anderson, 1975); and American Friends Service Committee, *Struggle for Justice* (New York: Hill and Wang, 1971).

3. National Institute of Corrections, *The Impact of Determinate Sentencing on Corrections* (Washington, D.C.: U.S. Department of Justice, 1980).

4. Reprinted by permission of *Family Weekly*, December 16, 1977, p. 1, copyright 1977, 641 Lexington Avenue, New York, N.Y., 10022.

5. Stephen Van Dine, Simon Dinitz, and John Conrad, "The Incapacitation of the Dangerous Offender: A Statistical Experiment," *Journal of Research in Crime and Delinquency* 14 (1977):22.

6. Beverly Koerin, "Violent Crime: Prediction and Control," *Crime and Delinquency* 24 (1978):58.

7. Ibid., p. 47.

8. Murray L. Cohen, A. Nicholas Groth, and Richard Siegal, "The Clinical Prediction of Dangerousness," *Crime and Delinquency* 24 (1978):30.

9. Stephen E. Schlesinger, "The Prediction of Dangerousness in Juveniles: A Replication," *Crime and Delinquency* 24 (1978):47.

10. John Monahan, "The Prevention of Violence," in *Community Mental Health and the Criminal Justice System,* ed. John Monahan (New York: Pergamon Press, 1976), p. 15.

11. Kurt Weis, "The Glueck Social Prediction Table: An Unfulfilled Promise," *Journal of Criminal Law and Crimonology* 65 (1964):397.

12. See Vincent O'Leary and Andrew von Hirsch, "Report of the Conference on Sentencing," mimeographed (School of Criminal Justice, State University of New York, Albany, 1975).

13. Norman Holt, "Rational Risk-Taking: Some Alternatives to Traditional Correctional Programs," in *Proceedings: Second National Workship on Corrections and Parole Administration* (College Park, Md.: American Correctional Association, 1974), p. 35.

14. Cohen, Groth, and Siegal, "Clinical Prediction of Dangerousness," p. 29.

15. Ernst A. Wenk, James O. Robison, and Gerald W. Smith, "Can Violence Be Predicted?" *Crime and Delinquency* 18 (1972):402.

16. Robert R. Hold, "Clinical and Statistical Prediction: A Reformulation and Some New Data," *Journal of Abnormal and Social Psychology* 56 (1958):1-12.

17. Cohen, Groth, and Siegel, "Clinical Prediction of Dangerousness," p. 31.

18. Vincent O'Leary and Daniel Glaser, "The Assessment of Risk in Parole Decision-Making," in *The Future of Parole: Commentaries on Systems in Britain and the U.S.,* ed. Donald J. West (London: Duckworth, 1972), p. 182.

19. Paul E. Meehl, *Clinical vs. Statistical Prediction* (Minneapolis; University of Minnesota Press, 1954), p. 222.

20. Theodore R. Sarbin, "A Contribution to the Study of Actuarial and Individual Methods of Prediction," *American Journal of Sociology* 48 (1943):601.

21. For a discussion of these studies, see Cohen, Groth, and Siegal, "Clinical Prediction of Dangerousness," and Schlesinger, "Prediction of Dangerousness in Juveniles."

22. Lloyd E. Ohlin, *Selection for Parole* (New York: Russell Sage, 1951), p. 69.

23. Ibid., p. 81.

24. See Don M. Gottfredson and Peter B. Hoffman, *Paroling Policy Guidelines: A Matter of Equity* (Davis, Calif.: National Council on Crime and Delinquency Research Center, 1973).

25. Hermann Mannheim and Leslie T. Wilkins, *Prediction Methods in Relation to Borstal Training* (London: Her Majesty's Stationery Office, 1955), p. 47.

26. Ibid.

27. Duane E. Brodchare, J.B. Ruark, and Douglas E. Scoven, "A Strategy for the Prediction of Work Release Success," *Criminal Justice and Behavior* 3 (1976):321.

28. Comptroller General of the United States, *State and County Probation: Systems in Crisis* (Washington, D.C.: Government Printing Office, 1976).

29. Ibid., p. 53.

30. Cohen, Groth, and Siegal, "Clinical Prediction of Dangerousness," p. 5. The studies were H.L. Kozol, R.S. Boucher, and R.F. Garofalo, "Diagnosis and Treatment of Dangerousness," *Crime and Delinquency* 18 (1972):371; and Emory F. Hodges, "Crime Prevention by the Indeterminate Sentencing Law," *American Journal of Psychiatry* 3 (1971):291.

31. See, for example, Gardner Lindsay, "Seer versus Sign," *Journal of Experimental Research in Personality* 1 (1965); and Roy Johnston and Benjamin F. McNeal, "Statistical versus Clinical Prediction: Length of Neuropsychiatric Hospital Stay," *Journal of Abnormal Psychology* 72 (1966): 335.

32. Paul E. Meehl, "A Comparison of Clinicians with Five Statistical Methods of Identifying Psychotic MMPI Profiles," *Journal of Counseling Psychology* 6 (1959):102.

33. Hold, "Clinical and Statistical Prediction," p. 15.

34. Quoted in Koerin, "Violent Crime," p. 52. See also, Stephen D. Gottfredson and Don M. Gottfredson, "Screening for Risk: A Comparison of Methods," *Criminal Justice and Behavior* 7 (1980):315.

35. S. Christopher Baird et al., "The Wisconsin Workload Project: A Two-Year Follow-Up Report," mimeographed (Wisconsin Department of Corrections, Madison, 1978).

36. Gottfredson and Gottfredson, *Decision-Making in Criminal Justice.*

37. For an example of this approach, see Systems and Communications Center, *The Iowa Offender Risk Assessment System,* Vol. 1: *System Coding Process* (Des Moines, 1980).

Part II
Implementation of
Risk Control

4

Risk Control and the Supervision Officer

We began our work in community-supervision agencies with the general idea that risk control should be the purpose of supervision. However, we had not yet developed specific strategies for making risk control operational at the line level of supervision. In working with community-supervision officers on a series of efforts, we recognized the need to develop a decision-making system to reinforce a structured risk-control focus at that level. What emerged was an objectives-based approach to case planning and supervision that facilitated risk-control judgments about offenders, identified supervision strategies to keep offenders out of trouble with the law, and created a means of reviewing, and thereby controlling, probation officers' exercise of discretion. This approach is based on the logic and principles of so-called systems planning.

Our first task was to introduce systems-oriented thinking to the community-supervision officer's world of work, the context in which the officer carries out his or her responsibilities, and then use this logic to structure that work context. The result was the objectives-based case-plan approach described in chapter 5.

The Work Context of the Supervision Officer

Typically, the supervision officer's work is described in prescriptive terms: a probation officer *should* be clinically skilled, with wide training in behavioral sciences;[1] or a parole officer *should* approach each client as an individual with unique needs and prospects.[2] According to much of the literature, supervision effectiveness is based primarily on personal characteristics, on the "officer's personality and the use he makes of it."[3] There is something akin to mysticism in a good deal of this thinking. In describing the work of the probation/parole officer, for example, Dressler has argued that "neither a social work method nor the skills connected with it can be imparted in a book."[4] The perceived need is for counselors who learn practical skills on the job and engage in the activity of therapeutic casework. However, in our interactions we frequently heard supervision officers express a degree of skepticism about their job similar to that found earlier among law-enforcement personnel.[5] Regardless of the attractiveness of the social-caseworker model, it is not uniformly accepted among supervision staff.[6]

The fact is that work realities shape the nature of the officer's job performance, regardless of a desire to be warm, accepting, professional, authoritative, or whatever other personal style the officer wishes to pursue. Officers clearly vary in the approaches that take to their work, but these variations are constrained by the overwhelming demands of the job itself.[7] As is true for most professional work, supervision of the offender has its own routine, contradictions, and repetitive aspects as well as opportunities for creative thinking and action. To attempt to understand this work by focusing solely on officer attributes and activities ignores the dynamics of the work that influence those attributes.

In our contact with line officers, we came to recognize that their work world consists of organizational routine and yet is also a system of processes and outputs. This understanding of the community-supervision function served as a starting point for our efforts to change the work they performed.

The concept of socio-technical systems, developed by E.L. Trist, emphasizes that the technology employed in a workplace represents a powerful and ultimately limiting force on the human organization in that workplace.[8] *Technology* refers to the means by which work is performed; in a supervision office it includes such methods as case-recording, job-development, surveillance and interviewing techniques. *Socio-technical* refers to the human systems that are organized to execute basic production technologies. In a probation office, these embrace such notions as the establishment of a caseload or the imposition of a pyramidal management system.

Attempts to change the behavior of individuals in any organization will fail if the socio-technical elements of that system are not recognized or altered.[9] The type of linear change described in chapter 1 (change derived by means of a self-contained system of logic and imposed from outside the context) fails more often than not because it does not account for the socio-technical aspects of organizations. Organic change, on the other hand, specifies the goals of change but develops the means of achieving them through interaction with those in an organization. This approach to change recognizes and accommodates the socio-technical system that is operative in the particular setting.[10] In our research efforts in community-supervision agencies, we attempted as much as possible to maintain an organic-change approach. Thus the socio-technical system existing in the offices where we carried out our work became increasingly the prime target of change rather than the attitudes, motivations, and personal attributes of staff, although the latter certainly could not be, and were not, ignored.

Our initial, academic understanding of socio-technical systems and of bureaucracies was based on an abstract view of the *potential* role the community-supervision sanction can play in criminal justice. The socio-technical-systems view of probation emerged as we acquired experience.

The task of structuring supervision activities forced us to come to grips with the nature of supervision as it operates on the line level of the organization.

The Themes of Supervision

Supervision agencies are professional "people-processing" organizations.[11] While this people processing is occurring, certain themes emerge around which supervision tasks come to be defined and organized. These dominant concepts, analogous to the core characteristics identified for police work and to lower-class "focal concerns,"[12] appear to color most, if not all, aspects of supervision decision making. Consequently, any attempt to reorganize supervision decision making must take them into account. The themes we have identified are not necessarily exhaustive; they are simply ways of labeling central concerns encountered by the officers with whom we worked. Additional themes may exist in other community-supervision settings. Moreover, not all officers in a community-supervision agency share the same values or have an equal emotional attachment to these themes; officers regard them with different intensity and accord them different significance. Regardless of individual officers' orientations, however, these themes permeate supervision decision making and are charged with importance for many of those with whom we worked.

Case Control

Offenders are typically organized into discrete caseloads, and each officer feels pressure to be in control of all cases assigned to him or her. In part, this is an issue of authority. The officer understandably wants clients to observe the imposed conditions of supervision and to comply with the agency's rules of conduct. The organizational importance of these rules and conditions has grown in recent years to the point that a recent national statement on probation defined the supervision function almost exclusively in terms of the enforcement of these requirements.[13]

But the probation/parole officer's concern for authority extends well beyond formal conditions to include day-to-day interactions with clients. Because community-supervision officers are given little direct power over the lives of their clients, they frequently must base the authority they carry on the credibility of their methods or the symbolism of their role. Obviously, these alternatives to significant power are effective only to the degree that officers are able to reinforce them either with personal behaviors that clients find credible (psychological authority) or with references to the client's current legal vulnerability and the officer's legitimate responsibility in that regard (symbolic authority).[14] These are not uniformly reliable tools for supervision, because they are heavily dependent on the client's responsiveness to supervision.[15]

Consequently, supervision officers expect—and, in some ways, need—their clients to readily accept their role as "client." Much of the early interaction between officers and clients is often designed to establish the ground rules of this authority-subservience relationship.[16] Robison and Takagi have found that, when possible, agencies impose significant sanctions on clients who refuse to accept this role.[17] The desire to establish authority in supervision is central to supervision officers' view of their work world. Frequently they will perceive experience with a client as satisfying when the latter has recognized their authority by responding to counseling and referrals and by expressing appreciation of their genuine assistance. At the other extreme is the clearly unsatisfying client who fails to accept any officer directives, rejects legitimate inquiries, and in general refuses to take seriously the status of being under supervision. Such a client has simply rejected the officer's authority.

This explains the extreme indignation with which some officers complain that judges and parole boards "won't back them up." The need for case control is central to the officer's satisfactory job performance—at least in terms of interactions with offenders. For clients with whom credibility-based authority techniques are ineffective, the absence of external support reinforces the limited symbolic authority of officers, forecloses the ability to establish control over clients, and, ultimately, limits the ability to perform the job and to obtain a measure of satisfaction in its accomplishment.

Of course, there are often good reasons why courts and parole boards refuse to "back up" officers' authority. Normally, the situation in which support becomes an issue is a violation hearing in which an officer alleges client misbehavior that falls short of a new criminal offense. The decision maker's reluctance to impose an incarcerative sanction on the basis of behaviors that are not ordinarily criminal but are merely violations of rules and conditions of supervision is understandable. Moreover, from the decision maker's point of view, the conditions were imposed precisely to assist the officer in requiring the client to comply with them. The violation often comes to be seen more as the officer's failure to enforce clear rules than as the client's failure to comply with them. The frequent result is that supervision is continued with an admonition from the decision maker that both parties "try a little harder."

The failure to achieve a desirable outcome in such tests of the officer's power exposes the officer's authority for what it really is: limited, fragile, and subject to the vagaries of external influences. The fact that the officer is often given responsibility for client functioning in areas over which he or she exercises little authority is a source of understandable frustration that leads to a sense of loss of control over cases.

This limitation of formal authority is offset by the fairly broad discretion an officer typically exercises over the supervision process. The officer retains a formidable array of intervention strategies, supervision styles, and techniques for establishing psychological authority over the client— including both the tone and substance of supervision—through discretionary approaches. The officer can be caring, distant, expository, non-directive, task centered, or otherwise, and can vary these approaches from client to client.[18]

Moreover, as we demonstrate in chapter 6, officers can also vary the number and type of supervision goals they establish for their clients. The variability in approaches to clients—which is extremely broad, even in the same office among the tightly knit, collegial officers—reflects in part the attitudes and beliefs the officer brings to the job. However, many seem to have a repertoire from which they select purposefully depending on the nature of the client. These officers appear to be more adept than their colleagues in using discretion as a tool for controlling their cases, altering their supervision approaches to suit the specifics of the client and client problems. And, as we show later and as others have documented,[19] some officers use this discretion in biased and potentially abusive ways.

Case-control concerns are also expressed in the way the officer prepares case records. Much case recording appears to be motivated less by a need to make the logic of the supervision effort explicit than to provide written documentation useful for parrying potential questions from a defense attorney at a violation hearing. It is through the case records that the officer in a sense prepares his or her argument that control of the case remained constant throughout supervision, and that the client's misbehavior was a result not of the officer's failure to supervise, but of the client's failure to respond appropriately to the supervision.

Thus, like everyone else, supervision officers take some of their self-image from the dynamics of their work. A central aspect of the officer's work is control, which includes the officer's capacity to influence the client's responsiveness to supervision. Understandably, the officer makes an effort to establish and maintain this control over the clients under supervision.

Case Management

A second set of concerns relates primarily to the officer's position as supervisor of a caseload. The traditional caseload structure in most organizations requires that the officer assume managerial responsibility for the workload.

Because the clients are not voluntary—their status is defined by external legal constraints and not by the services provided by the agency—the officer is more of a case manager than an ordinary caseworker, and many officers apparently come to view their work this way. As a result, paperwork routines predominate in decision making on cases: progress reports, regular case summaries, narrative reports of contacts, and special-event recording (such as violations or failures to report). Numerous studies of corrections supervision document the substantial portion of time spent in filling out forms.[20]

The requirements of paperwork create ambivalence among probation/parole personnel. Predictably, there is a general negativism toward completing reports because it is not a personally rewarding task. Frequently, officers consider the purpose of the forms vague or unimportant and resent the time it takes from that spent in direct contact with clients, an activity that is more personally satisfying.

But most probation officers also recognize that paperwork is the primary mechanism by which superiors can evaluate performance, and therefore it is important to give it some priority. Regular narrative reports fill a performance-evaluation vacuum: because there is very little way for a line supervisor to know *how well* an officer is doing in his work, there is a natural tendency to use case records as a means of knowing at least *what* the officer is doing. Therefore, officers often attempt to orient records to provide information on which performance can be assessed.

It is also true that paperwork is not as ambiguous as much of the regular work of the officer, so that it can provide a satisfying structured alternative to the vague and indefinite substantive tasks of supervision. Although it may be difficult to think of paperwork as job achievement, it at least offers the positive prospect of eventually being completed. As such, it is a task that provides the officer with closure, unlike much of the supervision officer's other routine work. Paperwork routine, then, becomes a core element of caseload management, perhaps because officers work with people who are often unpredictable and frequently experience crises. The work routine itself also helps to counteract the disruption common to the caseload. Consequently, officers often develop a structured week: one day (or more) designated as a field day, another day or two devoted only to office reports, a court day, and so forth. This kind of structure, by bringing a certain predictability to the officer's daily tasks, helps provide an element of stability to a caseload often in mayhem.

However, case-management structure also acts as a constraint on supervision methods. For example, an officer with a single weekly report day tends to supervise offenders accordingly, with monthly or bimonthly reporting requirements. Managing client reporting in this way also becomes a routine, and accordingly supervision activities sometimes flow more from the needs of the officer's work schedule than from the needs of the client. As the number of clients and complexity of client problems increase, so does the need for effective case management. In order to accommodate increased caseloads, agencies may identify subgroups of clients to be seen less frequently. But this new policy will require that officers justify variations in case reporting by the use of accurate, timely paperwork. As a result, paperwork routines for case management become a valuable asset for any supervision officer, frequent protestation to the contrary.

In the absence of an agency-wide system of caseload management (reporting routines, paperwork flow, and case-accounting techniques), most officers develop their own methods as a matter of simple necessity. Such idiosyncratic methods serve officers' needs reasonably well, but they do not necessarily serve the overall interests of the organization. Consequently, there has recently been an increased emphasis on systematized methods of caseload management.[21] These new, agency-wide systems often find themselves in competition with existing routines that officers have developed in order to deal with their managerial responsibilities. Even though the nature and degree of work required of the officer dictate a need for case management, the officer's approach to cases is often constrained by those case-management requirements.

Competence

The third major concern is more subtle than the others: many supervision officers question their capacity to exert a meaningful influence on their clients. This concern is commonly expressed as: "You can't help somebody unless he wants to be helped"; "Most of our people are losers to begin with, and they'll probably continue to be losers even if they make it off supervision"; "There's not much I can do if a person has made up his mind he wants to break the law"; "I never know whether the things I am doing with a client will ever really help him." Whether or not this verbal discounting is reasonable, it is of enormous significance in the psychology of supervision decision making. Line officers tend to suspect the effectiveness of their judgments about cases even though they may aggressively assert their professional expertise. This is true because there is almost no framework for understanding the appropriateness of supervision tasks beyond the formal supervision conditions and rules themselves, and the choices officers make sometimes fail and sometimes succeed. The result is that many officers develop a sense of limited competence in keeping their clients crime free.

Their perceptions may be at least partly accurate. Altering human behavior is a formidable and complex enterprise, one for which there are few experts and many pretenders. The hesitancy of officers is not necessarily inappropriate, especially given the limited time the officer has available to spend with each client.[22]

The significance of this concern about competence is not whether it is justified by the circumstances, but the fact that it exists. Almost all supervision officers are concerned that they not be held accountable for their clients' misbehaviors; that it be recognized that supervision choices are extremely limited and may well be ineffectual. The result is that officers are frequently unsure of their supervision strategies and vacillate widely in their approaches.

Officers sometimes learn a hard lesson from clients in whom they have developed a personal interest and invested emotional concern as well as supervision resources. When such a client fails—say, through a dramatic rearrest for a serious felony—the officer experiences cognitive and emotional incongruence: there is a sense of personal failure stemming from the client's failure. Yet some explanation for the event is necessary, and the easiest one is that the client did not respond to the officer's interventions, despite appearances to the contrary. Thus, the officer learns to distrust the positive responses of many clients almost as a defense mechanism.

This kind of response is intellectually generalizable: "How clients do on probation has less to do with supervision approaches than with the client's own motivations and desires, over which I have little influence." Experienced officers can help a new officer to overcome the psychological incongruence by putting the burden of failure on the client. Thus, even role socialization reinforces limited competence in supervision. The alternative—to believe that each officer is in fact responsible for the failures that occur among clients in his or her caseload—is clearly intolerable, from both the officer's point of view and that of the agency. Thus, the cynical view that clients determine their own outcomes, largely irrespective of probation, develops as a natural consequence of lack of meaningful feedback to officers.

Feedback in community supervision tends to operate as a sporadic negative-information device; officers seldom get clear confirmation that an approach they have used is effective. Those who successfully complete probation or parole are rearrested often enough to remind the officer not to place too much trust in terminations labeled "favorable adjustment." Sometimes even clients who are showing progress are suddenly rearrested. Officers are invariably made aware of their cases that fail; usually they must document and even handle the violation hearings themselves. Thus there is no standard source for positive feedback, and negative feedback is sporadic. Negative-feedback systems such as this cause staff to avoid obtaining feedback rather than to act on it once it comes.[23] Office norms often develop to neutralize officers from responsibility for the behaviors of their clients. If for no other motive than preservation of self-image, officers clients. If for no other motive than preservation of self-image, officers come to verbalize a lack of capacity to affect consistently the behavior choices of their clients. The result is that officers are sometimes almost surprised when one of their methods does work. Moreover, they are quick to adjust to their sense of limited ability as change agents, sliding from "theory to theory, technique to technique" when deciding how to handle clients.[24] Schnur recognized this sense of aimlessness in handling offenders when he stated that "almost all the objectives ever propounded and all the measures ever applied in dealing with the nonconformists since the beginning of time are employed today in the management of offenders."[25]

Although this eclectic philosophy might be appropriate for individual clients, as a normative expectation of all clients it is self-defeating. The belief that the way one does one's work is unrelated to the work product is an important source of burnout.[26] Beyond that, the expectation of limited competence allows officers to become lazy—if nothing works, why should they try very hard? Finally, it is self-fulfilling: an expectation that nothing can work helps ensure the adoption of strategies that indeed will not work.

This attitude is understandable, however. Given the nature of the clients, the community, and the job's reward structure, it is exceedingly difficult to resist doubts about supervision competence. Strategies that sometimes appear to work also sometimes fail, with no apparent difference between the situations. It is a disheartening situation. The realization of limited competence represented a career turning point for many of the officers with whom we worked.

In fact, what is surprising is that a number of officers are able to resist these organizational pressures toward cynicism. Despite the characteristics of the job, some officers maintain a sense of personal competence about supervision and decision making and possess a professional detachment about their work. Moreover, most of the officers we worked with sustained a belief in the importance of doing the job well, even if they felt that doing well was often not possible because of limitations in their clients, in the community, and in their agency.

Each of these three concerns powerfully affects the routines of supervision. They occupy much of the attention of the supervision officers and each officer's responses to them help to define his or her professional role.

Each of these themes also potentially constrains the officer's ability to pursue risk-control aims in supervision. Concern for control tends to override legitimate restrictions on the officer's discretion. Case-management routines often interfere with the officer's ability to select and implement appropriate risk-control interventions. Obviously, the greater the sense of incompetence, the greater the tendency to avoid actively supervising a case toward any utilitarian outcomes. Thus, any reform of the community-supervision function must address these concerns.

Bringing a Systems View to Supervision Routines

To respond to the work context of supervision, we developed a systems view of probation. The model we eventually adopted involved a series of considerations:

1. Differentiation of the results of supervision from the actitivities chosen to achieve those results
2. Emphasis on monitoring the intended results (goals) of supervision actions instead of only the actions taken by supervision staff
3. Systematic force-field analysis of the problems facing a client
4. Aggregation of supervision output data to establish an information system serving managerial and organizational needs
5. Emphasis on systematic planning at all levels in the organization, from line officer to supervisor to administrator
6. Provision of accurate feedback to line-supervisor administrative personnel to promote more effective use of resources at each level of the organization

Each of these elements was designed to resolve problems we faced in our effort to improve supervision.

The Problem of Effectiveness

The limited effectiveness of the general-caseload structure for supervision has been recognized for some time.[27] To address this problem, under funding of a general grant from the National Science Foundation we began to investigate the adaptability to supervision of various "teaming" methods devised in other social-service fields.[28] Teaming was felt to be an attractive alternative to traditional caseloads for several reasons, chiefly because it appeared to offer a better use of staff resources for supervising clients; the pooled expertise of staff would improve delivery of services.

   In our work with the probation staff, however, it soon became clear that this formulation of the problem was too narrow. There seemed to be a general feeling that the traditional caseload model was ineffective not so much because the structure was faulty, but because the effectiveness of supervision in general was problematic. The officers in our study asked incisive questions about the proposed team model: What will teaming help us to do better than we are doing now? What will it help us do differently? What evidence suggests that it fits our work better than some other approach? These questions eventually compelled us to abandon general, theoretical responses and to confront two facts: first, we had very little real idea of how a team operation would specifically alter the tasks and purposes of supervision from those of the traditional caseload structure; second—and more important—we were unable to recommend with confidence specific activities and strategies for supervising clients under any structure.

Consequently, we reoriented our research tasks. Instead of attempting to implement a new structure for supervision immediately, we turned to defining the type of structure best suited to the aims of supervision. This may seem to have been an obvious strategy, since it builds on a well-established systems principle: structure follows function. However, traditional caseload supervision more closely resembled the reverse—function follows structure; the caseload organization heavily influenced the way in which officers approached their work, partly because the organizational isolation of officers inhibited the establishment of a clear organizational purpose.[29]

In so doing, we addressed the problem as organizational in its broadest sense: How should we organize the various resources of supervision in order to improve its effectiveness? This perspective also raised a more fundamental question: What are the resources used in community supervision?

The Resources of Community Supervision

Most people familiar with community-supervision operations can enumerate the resources commonly used in the supervision process: referrals, individualized counseling, group counseling, and so on. Newman's general description of supervision reflects this common understanding:

> The treatment supervision process . . . entails the elaboration of knowledge about the individual through the process of communication, so that the individual will gain a more realistic appraisal of his own behavior thereby enhancing his own ability to function more acceptably in the community. The provision of certain material services may also be involved in the treatment process.[30]

One apparently logical approach would be to determine how traditional caseload methods utilize these resources (staff time, counseling, referrals, and direct services) so that service delivery might be reorganized to improve the allocation and use of these resources. This strategy, though, is not helpful, because the current use of resources under the traditional caseload is more a function of the caseload structure than of the unique nature of the clients and their needs. Newman's description of supervision resources tends to be used on all clients, regardless of their situation or level of risk. Consequently, a simple restructuring of this approach is not helpful. Our officers put it this way: "We already know the kinds of things we are trying to do with our cases. But we use counseling and job referrals because that's what we know how to do. What we need to find out is what we *should* be doing with a case, and that may not be the same as what we are now doing."

In fact the focus on traditional supervision activities contributes to many of the problems facing probation and parole officers. One reason is that selection of supervision activities occurs in the context of what Thompson refers to as technical "uncertainty"; the outputs of various technological alternatives are not fully predictable.[31] Thus, probation and parole officers often select activities without having a firm idea of their probable results. Consequently, they often choose activities not because of their intended results, but simply because they are commonly used and are available. Probation and parole officers frequently engage in counseling with clients primarily because they can do it, and not necessarily because counseling has potential usefulness in resolving a specific problem. Counseling is a readily available resource. Similarly, referral to external agencies often becomes a routine response to a perceived client need, regardless of whether that need is centrally related to the offender's risk of criminal behavior, whether the client perceives the need as a problem, and whether the agency of referral is competent or willing to deal with it. The use of resources in probation and parole is frequently haphazard, unorganized, and unplanned.

The usefulness of a supervision approach that applies a set of identical resources to all offenders is at best questionable, given the overwhelming evidence that such global prescriptions are "a disservice to the individuals subjected to them."[32] Research results indicate that indiscriminate-treatment programs have "helped some, hurt some, and had no effects on others."[33] Nevertheless, group counseling for everyone is common in community supervision, and there are widespread claims that the goals of supervision for all clients are basically the same.

As might be expected, this wholesale approach has adverse effects on the supervision effort. Perhaps most important is the fact that using resources in this unconsidered way lowers staff morale. In the context of sporadic negative feedback, officers routinize the use of resources and thereby confirm their experience that the application of resources to clients is normally fruitless, or at best irrelevant to client adjustment to supervision. When resources are used without regard for their appropriateness in preventing criminality, the connection between resources and supervision outcomes—defined in terms of legal behaviors—becomes even more tenuous.

This cycle constitutes a recipe for burnout. Staff focus their time and attention on the application of resources to cases. Performance evaluation of staff and agency self-assessment—to the degree that they occur at all—are often based on the energy with which resources (in quantity and variety) are employed, especially personal contacts and referrals. Churchman has commented on the inappropriateness of this approach: "one cannot use the amount of physical activity as a measure of the performance of a system. One has to show that activity is translated into a measure of utility or value."[34]

Yet there is little consistent relation between case outcomes and effort expended and resources employed; all experienced officers can tell of cases to which they devoted tremendous effort, only to see the client later rearrested and sentenced to prison. It is a discouraging situation, and the officer comes somewhat understandably to feel that the harder he or she works, the less the work appears to translate into results.

Odiorne has referred to this phenomenon as the "activity trap," and others have discussed its contribution to job dissatisfaction.[35] In community supervision, this focus on activities (expenditure of resources) is exemplified by treatment plans (and presentence investigations) that detail only the referrals to be made and problems to be counseled, not results to be achieved; or in periodic case reports that represent a simple chronicle of activities instead of results.

There is one advantage to the focus on activities in supervision: it increases the officer's sense of control over the case. By taking actions on cases, officers (and the agency) can feel they are aggressively supervising the client, especially if the client is responsive to the officer's use of resources. However, this focus on resources is a double-edged sword: it may also exacerbate the officer's perception of supervision as being largely ineffective.

Management theorists suggest that a solution to this problem of activity focus is to develop instead an emphasis on results.[36] In general, a result orientation requires a person to obtain a clear idea of the intended outcomes of an action before undertaking it. The value of an action—or resource application—is based on the utility of its intended outputs. This is the essence of a systems approach to resource planning—clarifying results of actions before taking them.[37]

In working with officers, we came to recognize the futility of focusing on resource specification as the basic step in organizational decisions and began to explore ways of specifying supervision outcomes before identifying resources for supervision. From approaching supervision decision making as a *reactive* process of responding to client incidents and problems, we came to approach it as a *proactive* function of analyzing and planning the supervision of a case. The intention was to identify the resources that are *appropriate* to a given case prior to applying them.

Identifying Resource Appropriateness

Two factors require that community supervision use its resources with caution in supervising clients. One is the scarcity of resources. Recently, classification systems have been devised to identify clients requiring less time and attention from officers so that resources can be concentrated offenders who most clearly require supervision.[38] With growing caseloads and reduced referral resources, supervision agencies have to decide which cases will receive priority. Consequently, one aspect of the appropriateness of supervision resources is the degree to which the client receiving them represents a higher priority than others who are not receiving resources.

The scarcity of resources raises the second issue in their application—to what general purpose are they being applied? That is, on what basis will clients be assessed as to their relative priority for receiving scarce resources?

Since the inception of community supervision, there has been debate about whether its primary purpose is to provide social services or community protection.[39] The ambiguous relationship of community supervision agencies to executive or judicial branches of government has compounded the difficulty of establishing a clear purpose.[40] Ambivalence in purpose has also plagued recent attempts to write "model" mission statements.[41]

Our own experience confirmed the existence of this ambivalence. On the one hand, many officers felt a humane desire to help offenders try to resolve all their problems. These officers saw the central aim of supervision to be delivery of service and tended to apply resources to clients whenever there appeared to be a need. Other officers allocated resources on the basis of the client's criminal behavior, justifying supervision in terms of the client's past and potential criminality. Other probation officers were court-service oriented and allocated resources primarily with a view to enforcing court-ordered conditions.

Thus the definition of appropriate use of resources for a given client differs according to the officer's orientation to purpose. For example, a low-risk offender with many personal problems and one or two court conditions would be handled very differently by each officer. Under a services-oriented philosophy, this offender would receive much attention. The crime-oriented officer would do very little with this case because of the slight risk the offender poses. The court-oriented officer would take only the actions necessary to enforce the conditions for the client. Clearly, to determine the appropriateness of resource allocation, the agency must initially determine the purpose to which it is applying its resources.

We have argued in earlier chapters that community supervision ought to be directed to achieving constrained risk control. Under this model, a resource is appropriate if (1) it is selected because the offender's risk to the community is such that attention to the case is required, and (2) there is some reasonable likelihood that the intervention strategy selected will control or reduce the risk, so long as (3) the resource does not constitute a more severe intervention into the client's life than is justified by the seriousness of the offense. Although other purposes also have potential merit, this model provides definite advantages, discussed earlier.

Our identification of control as the guiding principle of supervision was a product of lengthy discussion and argument among the officers and researchers. The essential logic of our discussions was:

1. The clients do not seek services voluntarily.
2. The decisionmaker (judge or parole board) is not in a position to make reasoned decisions about the specific resources needed by the client (as evidenced by the frequent inappropriateness of supervision conditions).
3. The justification for community supervision resides in its capacity to minimize efficiently and effectively the criminality of those assigned to its jurisdiction.

As we have defined it, the risk-control function of supervision is also a limiting principle. The decision to apply a resource to a client constitutes an intervention into that client's life and therefore requires careful consideration. The burden is on the officer to justify the intervention (resource) decisions. Our criterion for the choice of intervention was the resource's potential for increasing law-abiding behavior; this criterion emphasizes positive outcomes. Thus, a resource is appropriate if it is associated with a risk-reducing outcome by increasing law-abiding behavior (while not violating the principles described in part I).

Specifying Supervision Outcomes

Fundamental to the purposeful use of resources in supervising clients is the capacity to specify intended outcomes. This means that the officer must identify desired outcomes early in the supervision period. We asked our officers to specify the outcomes they were trying to achieve in terms of *changes* in the client. Their answers were often vague or ambiguous: "increased maturity," "ability to deal with authority," "improved self-image." This ambiguity made it clear that we needed to rethink the traditional conceptualization and language of community supervision. Like most social-service workers, the officers tended to frame the substance of their work in terms of broad attitudinal or otherwise nonspecific changes. Unkovik's description of the treatment objectives for a training school provides an example:

1. Guiding the delinquent child to develop a healthy and wholesome personality for his life in the adult world.
2. Helping the child in his successful adjustment to accept societal norms of behavior and to form effective relationships with other persons.
3. Developing the delinquent child into a knowledgeable and participating member of society, vocationally and culturally.[42]

These objectives are difficult to define operationally because they are subject to individual judgment: one officer's definition of a "knowledgeable and participating member of society" might be identical to another officer's definition of overly aggressive and antiauthoritarian behavior. The vagueness of these objectives makes it difficult to determine the appropriateness of the use of resources in any given case.

We wanted to pinpoint supervision objectives that could be used to control officer discretion, identify appropriate resources, and evaluate the client's performance under supervision. To serve these functions, an objective must be specific and (at least technically) measurable. With an objective such as "to obtain full-time employment within three weeks" it is easier to determine its appropriateness as a risk-control aim and to assess the client's achievement of the objective.

From the variety of approaches available for articulating objectives, we selected a model commonly used in education—behavioral objectives. This model seemed most adaptable to the probation setting because it could be used to identify the specific intended aims of supervision in terms of *behavioral* change in the client. We chose a behavioral focus because we recognized that:

> Offenders are offenders because of their present behavior. Then the task becomes that of asking what facet or facets of this person's behavior is critical for his having become an offender. . . . We can evaluate corrections on the basis of the extent to which it succeeds, in the correctional setting, in changing those behaviors which it has set out to change.[43]

For each objective, the officer could indicate a specific resource (intervention) to be used to assist the client achieving the objective, and the appropriateness of the objective became the standard for testing the appropriateness of the resource.

The systems approach we developed for planning a client's community supervision has four essential steps:

1. Determining the degree of supervision emphasis (and coercion) a client should receive, depending on the risk level represented by that client
2. Analyzing the problems that affect the client's risk to the community
3. Specifying the client's behavioral objectives in order to control risk
4. Specifying resources (techniques or interventions) to be used in regard to each objective

To emphasize the proactive nature of this approach, we devised a format called the Program Plan Profile (PPP). Appendix A presents a sample form. In chapter 5 we provide a detailed description of the model, published elsewhere under the title *Objectives-based Case Planning*.[44]

Systems Approaches and Routines

Substantively, there is little unique in this approach to supervision planning. Several models have been devised that rely on the idea of objectives.[45] "Task-centered casework," the notion of breaking down casework interaction into specific client tasks, has been applied in a number of social-service settings.[46] A number of recent innovations in risk prediction have established supervision priorities.[47] Finally, systematic analysis of clients needs has characterized several client-supervision approaches.[48] The elements of our approach represent the collapsed logic of most standard planning approaches.

However, this model is different in two ways. First, it was developed through the joint efforts of researchers and community-supervision staff in a multiyear organizational-developmental project. Thus, it was not a product of abstract academic reasoning—or static principles of administration. Instead, this approach resulted from what might be called organic logic: each stage of the research constituted a learning experience, and various possibilities were tested until the final model was established. Thus, it represents the pooled knowledge of practicing officers and academic researchers.

The second distinctive aspect flows from the first. Perhaps as a result of the officers' involvement, the model proved relevant to the problems of community supervision described at the beginning of this chapter. Although no model can ever solve all the problems of supervision work—they are, to a degree, endemic to the supervision function—this objectives-based approach appears to reduce some of the negative effects.

The community-supervision concern about *competence,* for example, stems in part from the fact that most supervision interventions are reactive and thus have limited potential for achieving the purposes of supervision. Moreover, many of the interventions typically chosen are not the product of careful reasoning, but instead reflect the routine approaches of the officer. Systematic case planning overcomes this problem by forcing the officer to consider the client-specific aims of supervision in light of the general purpose of risk control. This makes resource allocation (interventions) purposeful rather than routine. In addition, the objectives-based structure creates a potential for positive feedback to augment the existing sporadic negative-feedback system, thus reducing the pervasive sense of ineffectiveness that emerges from negative feedback. In assessing the client's progress under supervision, the officer can learn in a systematic way when his or her efforts have assisted the client in achieving the behavioral goals established as significantly related to the client's risk. Thus, successful supervision need no longer leave the officer in a feedback void. Moreover, the objectives-based case-planning model is grounded in casework approaches that have been shown to be more effective because they specify tasks and use joint behavior contracting between the client and the officer.[49]

The objectives-based case plan has the potential for facilitating appropriate control over the client in two ways. First, the officer is able to differentiate the role of supervision conditions (which the officer must enforce simply by virtue of their imposition by a legal authority) from risk-control supervision objectives (which are a product of officer-client interaction). The approach that officers take in establishing objectives for clients can tolerate a variety of styles, from total involvement of the client to simple, unidirectional objectives setting. The approach may be varied according to the offender's responsiveness to supervision. Consequently, the officer can use the fact that a written case plan is required to ensure that the client be responsive to the risk-control effort.

Second, the case plan provides a basis for making judgments about the client's supervision status. Client performance on supervision objectives can play an important role in determining the agency's recommendation regarding the continuation of supervision, should the client be rearrested or face technical violation for failure to comply with conditions. Progress shown by offenders on objectives provides a justification for continuing their supervision status; offenders not showing progress demonstrate by their prior behavior the futility of continued supervision. A written record makes the client's performance visible and available to decision makers in authority. It is easier for these decision makers to follow the recommendations of the supervision agency when such recommendations are supported by documents that identify specific behavioral characteristics of the client.

Case planning is also related to *case management* in obvious ways. It helps the officer determine the frequency of contacts (based partly in the degree of risk); it provides a structure for determining when a case is ready for reduced reporting and (ultimately) termination; and it establishes a basis for allocation of supervision resources. Most important, the case plan establishes a logical structure for approaching cases that takes into account the unpredictabilities of client behavior without eliminating the scheduled regularity the officer needs to manage the necessary work.

Systematic Case Planning and Administration

So far, we have emphasized the benefits of our model from the perspective of the line officer. This emphasis developed because we worked with line officers in designing the approach to supervision planning. However, the greatest potential benefit of systematic planning with supervision objectives may lie in its capacity for monitoring the discretion of officers and assisting agency administration. In later chapters we show how supervision-objectives data can be used to make visible decisions and address organizational problems. Compiled in an information system, case-plan data provide the administrator with an invaluable source of information for monitoring, planning and problem solving.

This administrative potential is predicated on the fact that officers find the data useful for their own work and therefore record information that is accurate. Large, centralized data systems that rely on information produced by line officers (who complete most of the paperwork manually) often unintentionally reward officers for providing data in a haphazard way. Because the data often are never fed back to the line officer, officers tend to complete the forms with a minimum of time and attention. Too often the result is inaccurate information. In one instance of which we are aware, a large centralized system that cost about $500,000 to install was able to produce only six-month-old caseload printouts that were about 50-percent accurate. Under these circumstances, no officer felt it necessary to supply accurate information on input documents. By using information directly from case plans, however, administators increase the officer's expertise and need to compile meaningful plans.

Summary

In this chapter we have discussed a socio-technical systems approach to structuring the day-to-day office tasks of the supervision officer. This systems approach was based on the view of supervision we developed during a series of projects designed to improve the use of resources in supervision.

We found that the work world of the line-supervision officer is dominated by three concerns. First, the officer is concerned about *case control*—the client's responsiveness to supervision and the officer's ability to call on legal actors to support his or her decision making. Second, in the face of growing caseloads and expanding paperwork, the officer has a legitimate concern about *case management*. Finally, the officer is concerned about his or her *competence* in choosing strategies for clients. Competence is constrained by limited knowledge about supervision effectiveness, a sporadic negative-feedback system, and frustrations in dealing with difficult clients.

These concerns led us to adopt a systems approach to supervision decision making. This approach includes analysis of the risk posed by the offender and of the problems that create that risk, the specification of objectives to resolve those problems, and the identification of resources to help the offender achieve the objectives. In addition to structuring the line-officer's work routines, this system provides an excellent source of data for administrative decision making and controlling discretion.

Notes

1. See, for example, Robert H. Dalton, "Value and Use of Counseling Techniques in the Work of Probation Officers," *Federal Probation* 4, no. 4 (1952):17-22.

2. See, for example, Charles L. Newman, "Concepts of Treatment in Probation and Parole Supervision," *Federal Probation* 25, no. 1 (1961): p. 38.

3. Edmond G. Burbank and Ernest W. Goldsboro, "The Probation Officer's Personality: A Key Factor in Rehabilitation," *Federal Probation* 18, no. 2 (1954):12

4. David Dressler, *Practice and Theory of Probation and Parole* (New York: Columbia University Press, 1969).

5. See, for example, Arthur Neiderhoffer, *Behind the Shield: The Police in Urban Society* (Garden City, N.Y.: Doubleday, 1967); and Herman Goldstein, *Policing a Free Society* (Cambridge, Mass.: Ballinger, 1977).

6. This realization is contained in a number of discussions of probation and parole supervision, including David T. Stanley, *Prisoners among Us: The Problem of Parole* (Washington, D.C.: Brookings Institution, 1977); Executive Advisory Committee on Sentencing, *Crime and Punishment in New York* (New York, 1979); and Elliot Studt, *Surveillance and Service in Parole Supervision* (Los Angeles: University of California at Los Angeles, 1969).

7. See Michael Lipsky, *Street-Level Bureaucracy: Dilemmas of the Individual in Public Services* (New York: Russell Sage, 1980).

8. E.L. Trist, "On Socio-Technical Systems," in Kenneth D. Benne, and Robert Chin, 2d ed. Warren Bennis, *The Planning of Change,* (New York: Holt, Rinehart and Winston 1969).

9. See Daniel Katz and Robert Kahn, *The Social Psychology of Organizations* (New York: Wiley, 1969).

10. See Chris Argyris, *Integrating the Individual and the Organization* (New York: Wiley, 1964).

11. For a discussion of this; see Charles Suchar, *Social Deviance: Problems and Prospects* (New York: Holt, Rinehart and Winston, 1978).

12. For a discussion of core characteristics of police work, see Jerome Skolnick, *Justice without Trial: Law Enforcement in a Democratic Society* (New York: Wiley, 1966), especially the discussion of authority/danger; for lower-class "focal concerns," see Walter B. Miller, "Lower Class Culture as a Generating Milieu of Gang Delinquency, *Journal of Social Issues* 14 (Summer 1958): 5-19.

13. David Fogel, "A Call to Action," mimeographed (University of Illinois-Chicago Circle, 1981).

14. Shankar Yelaja, ed., *Authority and Social Casework,* (Toronto: University of Toronto Press, 1971).

15. See John Klofas and David Duffee, "The Change Grid and the Active Client" *Criminal Justice and Behavior,* 8 (1981); and Ted Palmer, "Martinson Revisited," *Journal of Research in Crime and Delinquency* 21 (1975):133.

16. Carl B. Klockars, "A Theory of Probation Supervision," *Journal of Criminal Law, Criminology, and Police Science* 63 (1972):550-57.

17. James Robison and Paul Takagi, "The Parole Violator as an Organizational Reject," in *Probation, Parole, and Community Corrections,* eds. Robert M. Carter and Leslie T. Wilkins (New York: Wiley, 1976), pp. 347-67.

18. Gary Arling and Ken Lerner, *Client Management Classification* (Washington, D.C.: National Institute of Corrections, 1981).

19. See Andrew von Hirsch and Kathleen J. Hanrahan, *The Question of Parole, Retention, Reform, or Abolition?* (Cambridge, Mass.: Ballinger, 1979).

20. Arthur P. Miles, "Time Studies in Probation and Parole," *Crime and Delinquency* 15 (1969):260.

21. For example, the National Institute of Corrections has made case management in field services a priority area for funding; see *Annual Plan, 1981,* and *Annual Plan, 1982* (Washington, D.C.).

22. See, for example, Virginia Department of Probation and Parole Services, "Results of Probation/Parole Officers Time Study," mimeographed (Virginia Department of Corrections, Richmond, 1976).

23. Douglas McGregor, *The Professional Manager* (New York: McGraw-Hill, 1967), pp. 123-27.

24. Scott Briar, "Effective Social Work Intervention in Direct Practice: Implications for Education" (Paper presented at the meeting of the Council for Social Work Education, San Francisco, February 1973), p. 3.

25. Alfred Schnur, "Some Reflections on the Role of Correctional Research," *Law and Contemporary Problems* 32 (1958):722.

26. Cary Cherness, *Professional Burnout in Human Service Organizations* (New York: Praeger, 1980).

27. Mark A. Niethercutt and Don M. Gottfredson, *Case Load Size Variation and Difference in Probation and Parole Performance* (Washington, D.C.: National Center for Juvenile Justice, 1975).

28. Naomi I. Brill, *Teamwork: Working Together in the Human Services* (Philadelphia: Lippincott, 1976).

29. P. Kevin Benoit and Todd R. Clear, "Case Management Systems in Probation," mimeographed (Training Center, National Council on Crime and Delinquency, Hackensack, N.J., 1980).

30. Charles L. Newman, "Concepts of Treatment in Probation and Parole Supervision, *Federal Probation* 25, no. 1 (1961):40. Reprinted with permission from *Federal Probation Quarterly,* March 1961.

31. James D. Thompson, *Organizations in Action* (New York: McGraw-Hill, 1967).

32. Marguerite Q. Warren, "Intervention with Juvenile Delinquents," in *Pursuing Justice for the Child*, ed. Rosenheim (Chicago: University of Chicago Press, 1975), pp. 4-5.

33. Marguerite Q. Warren, "All Things Being Equal . . .," *Criminal Law Bulletin* 9 (1973):482.

34. C. West Churchman, *The Systems Approach* (New York: Dell, 1968), p. 108. See also Gerald M. Weinberg, *An Introduction to Systems Thinking* (New York: Wiley-Interscience, 1975).

35. George Odiorne, *Management and the Activity Trap* (New York: Harper & Row, 1974); Cary Cherniss, *Staff Burnout: Job Stress in the Human Services* (Palo Alto, Calif.: Sage, 1980).

36. William C. Reif and Gerald Bassford, "What MBO Really Does," *Business Horizons*, June 1973, pp. 1-8.

37. See Vincent O'Leary, "Reflections on the Systems Age in Corrections" (Paper presented at the meeting of the National Conference on Criminal Justice, Washington, D.C., January 1973).

38. S. Christopher Baird et al., "The Wisconsin Workload Project: Two-Year Follow-up Report," mimeographed (Wisconsin Department of Corrections, Madison, 1978).

39. Todd R. Clear, "Three Dilemmas in Community Supervision," *Prison Journal* 59 (Autumn-Winter 1979):3-16.

40. General Accounting Office, *State and County Probation: Systems in Crisis* (Washington, D.C.: Government Printing Office, 1976).

41. See, for example, Fogel, "A Call to Action," and New Jersey Administrative Office of the Courts, "The Mission of Probation in New Jersey," mimeographed (Trenton, 1981).

42. Charles M. Unkovic and William J. Ducsay, "Objectives of Training Schools for Delinquents," *Federal Probation* 33, (1969):50.

43. Herbert C. Quay, "What Corrections Can Correct and How," *Federal Probation* 37, no. 2 (1973): pp. 3, 5. Reprinted with permission from *Federal Probation Quarterly*, June 1973.

44. Todd R. Clear, *Objectives-based Case Planning* (Washington, D.C.: National Institute of Corrections, 1981).

45. See, for example, Al Havenstrite, "Case Planning in the Probation Supervision Process," *Federal Probation* 44, no. 2 (1980):57-66.

46. William J. Reid and Laura Epstein, *Task-centered Casework* (New York: Columbia University Press, 1972).

47. Marvin Bornstedt et al., *Classification for Field Services* (Washington, D.C.: National Institute of Corrections, 1980).

48. See Baird et al., "Wisconsin Workload Project."

49. William J. Reid and Laura Epstein, eds., *Task-Centered Practice* (New York: Columbia University Press, 1977); Paul Gendreau and Bob Ross, "Effective Correctional Treatment: Bibliotherapy for Cynics," *Crime and Delinquency* 25 (1979):463-89.

5 The Objectives-Based Case Record

This chapter presents the objectives-based case-diagnostic and planning method for supervision developed in the probation projects summarized earlier. The approach includes four steps, which are listed below with their rationale.

1. *Risk Classification:* Specifying the supervision requirements of the case according to the appropriate level of risk control serves to set outer limits on appropriate intervention levels during supervision.
2. *Analysis of Key Forces:* Creating an array of crime-related forces in a case establishes a basis for identifying and selecting key intervention points.
3. *Specification of Objectives:* Identifying a set of measurable and specific intended outcomes of the supervision process in terms of behavioral objectives makes supervision discretion visible by identifying its purposes and provides information on areas for supervision that can be used to identify case-management priorities.
4. *Specification of Resources*: Specifying the intervention method (resource) to be used to achieve each of the supervision objectives provides information on the availability and appropriate use of resources.

Risk Classification

As we indicated in chapter 3, the first and perhaps crucial tasks in a risk-control system are to classify the offender in terms of the risk posed and to assign the client to the program that will best manage the risk. Classification decisions are most reliable when they include use of a validated risk-assessment instrument. A number of these already exist,[1] but there is conflicting evidence on the degree to which they generalize to different populations,[2] and none of them appears to be sufficiently effective to warrant uniform adoption.[3] Ideally, each jurisdiction should generate its own prediction model based on its own clients and routinely update the model over time.

The classification system suggested in chapter 3 was designed for sentencing offenders initially to various broadly defined content levels. That general model needs to be augmented for the propose of risk management within those categories. Thus in table 5-1 we outline a model for a

Table 5-1
Sample Probation-Classification Model

Type	Risk Score	Reconviction Rate (percentage)	Type of Initial Program Expected
I	0-5	6.3	Minimum community supervision
	6-10	10.2	
II	11-15	28.9	Regular community supervision
	16-20	46.4	
III	21-25	63.2	Intensive community supervision
	26-31	76.5	

probation-supervision agency. In the table the risk scores range from 0 to 31. The third column shows the history of reconviction for offenders in these risk-score categories. On the basis of this risk score, an offender would be placed in one of three classes, each indicating the appropriate type of initial program assignment. Variations in initial assignments would be possible but would have to be explained.

Because no statistical system was available to us for developing techniques of behavioral specification, we used the system shown in table 5-2 to classify cases. This crude classification system, though a mix of risk- and non-risk-control elements and thus less sophisticated than the system described above, provided insight into practical possibilities for developing the technology of classification and a good deal of information about the number of probation cases likely to be assigned to various categories. In the six court systems in which we first developed this classification system, we found officers classifying supervision levels according to the categories shown in table 5-3. Approximately one-fourth of the cases were considered to require intensive intervention by the state, and another one-fourth minimal intervention.

Under the system we designed, probation officers saw the clients assigned to level 1 only about once every six months. Probationers were required only to fill out monthly reports to maintain contact with the court and were supervised largely through surveys of police-department arrest records or records of support payment and restitution. Probation officers supervising level-1 cases handled as many as 300 or 400 clients apiece. The punishment purposes of the state were met and intervention in the lives of offenders was minimal indeed.

Clients in level 2 were probationers who received regular supervision. For this level, we developed a system of team supervision among probation officers with very close networks in the community. Although probationers

Table 5-2
Classification System Using Risk- and Non-Risk-Control Elements

Program Indicated by Level of Risk	Client Characteristics
Level 1: Minimum community supervision	Client does not now pose a significant threat to the public, no requirements of the court call for close supervision, and client has no important problems that are specifically related to potential serious violations of the law and that the probation service can reasonably expect to affect substantially.
Level 2: Regular community supervision	Client does not pose a significant threat to the public, and no close supervision is mandated by the court; but client is currently coping with a significant set of problems related to potential violations of the law. Client has some expectation of overcoming these problems with the assistance of the probation service.
Level 3: Intensive community supervision	Client has been recently assigned to probation and has a history of violent behavior toward others or is likely to commit a fairly serious violation of the law, or the requirements imposed by the court can be enforced only by close and persistent supervision.

had to meet rules and report more frequently than those in level 1, no participation in a treatment program was required, and primary reliance was on programs provided by other agencies. The focus in level 2 was on resource development in the community and service to the probationers.

Probation officers supervising level-3 cases had very small caseloads, and the objectives were essentially incapacitative; probationers were held to very strict rules and were seen very frequently. After six months, a probationer assigned to level 3 was automatically moved to level 2 unless a valid reason could be given for retaining the probationer in level 3. Similarly, a client was moved from level 2 to level 1 at a specified time unless a compelling reason could be given for not doing so. Any probationer who was moved down a category, from 1 to 2, or from 2 to 3, had the right to a review of the decision in a neutral forum.

Table 5-3
Supervision Levels of Cases in Six Courts

Level	Type of Supervision	Number of Cases
1	minimum supervision	261
2	regular supervision	609
3	intensive supervision	259

Within this framework, probation officers retained tremendous discretion. The next task thus became that of helping probation officers perform their jobs in a way that made that discretion susceptible to review. Behavioral objectives could serve this purpose, but before officers can articulate meaningful objectives, they must have an appropriate means of analyzing a case to develop a foundation for those objectives. A number of such analytical systems have been developed; the system described below is representative of one type.

Analysis of Key Forces

The interventions used in probation must be directed to problems that interfere with the offender's ability to live in the community without breaking the law. In a risk-control model, it is imperative that the focus of intervention remain on that objective.

Aside from some studies suggesting that employment and (with more ambivalent results) financial support are related to successful supervision,[4] little is known about what factors and problems are actually linked to prevention of new crimes. This dearth of information makes it difficult to maintain a focus on promoting crime-free living. In the absence of such knowledge, a systematic technique must be used for identifying potentially crime-related problems. The technique we adapted to community supervision is Kurt Lewin's force-field analysis.[5] As originally developed by Lewin, force-field analysis was both a means of analyzing why an event occurs in society and a technique for planning how to modify the frequency of the occurrance of that event.

Lewin argued that any social event in a stated social group can be visualized as occurring at a given frequency. The frequency will be determined by various forces acting on the social event, some of which lead to an increased frequency, and others having the opposite effect. For example, the availability of handguns would tend to increase the frequency of violent crime. An event occurs at a given frequency at a given time because the forces acting on it have attained a "semi-stable equilibrium"; that is, the total strength of the forces tending to increase its frequency is roughly equal to the total strength of the forces decreasing its frequency. An event shows a steady pattern of change in frequency because the forces determining frequency are themselves changing steadily. Thus, it is possible to describe a given phenomenon or event in terms of an array of the forces that surround it. Figure 5-1 presents force-field analysis of violent crime, when the purpose of the analysis is to reduce the general amount of violent crime in a community. This example does not provide an exhaustive set of forces, but it illustrates both how a force field is constructed and how key forces can be

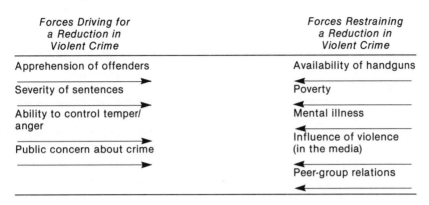

Figure 5-1. A Partial Force-Field Analysis of Violent Crime

selected in a change effort. In general, change is achieved by increasing *driving* forces, decreasing *restraining* forces, or both. Thus the target of change is not the event of violent crime itself, but the forces that determine its frequency. In selecting the target forces, four guidelines can be used:

1. *Strength:* forces that play an important role in determining the frequency of the event
2. *Alterability:* forces for which means exist to change the degree or nature of their influence on the event
3. *Speed:* forces that can be manipulated quickly
4. *Interdependency:* forces that are crucial in the sense that a change in them will have an influence on many other forces

The fact that a force meets one or two of these guidelines does not automatically make it a change target. Rather, it is the interaction of these guidelines that helps to determine target forces in any change effort. For example, many writers have stressed the theoretical relationships between level of crime and certainty of apprehension (strength), but given the nature of violent crime, there are finite limits on the ability of the police to apprehend offenders (alterability). On the other hand, the availability of handguns may be a strong force that is also relatively easy to change through economic and legal reforms. Although poverty may be a heavily interdependent force in this case, since it is linked to several other forces, changing this factor is likely to be a long process.

Finally, the force-field method suggests that to achieve the maximum effect, the change agent should work on both sides of the force field. The temptation is always to add driving forces for the change (by passing new laws or threatening punishments), but the addition of forces creates more tension in the system. The longest-lasting changes are those achieved without a net increase in total forces on the system, by achieving a reduction in resisting forces to complement increases in driving forces.

A probation officer can perform a more comprehensive force-field analysis of the change tasks presented by an individual under probation supervision in the community. In such a case, the objective of the analysis is to increase the amount of law-abiding behavior. The forces that exist in the client and in his or her environment can then be arrayed in a force field in terms of their relationships to law-abiding behavior.

Consider the characteristics of a fictitious client, Henry Ward. Ward is a nineteen-year-old brought before the court on a second-degree assault—a fight with an acquaintance. He has four prior arrests, one for auto theft resulting in three years on juvenile probation. Henry has a ninth-grade education and a sporadic employment record. His school performance has been poor and he expresses little interest in pursuing his education. Henry now lives with his mother but has a steady relationship with a girlfriend, Diane. His psychological evaluation indicates that he is immature and quick-tempered but has severe emotional problems. His relationship with his mother has been ambivalent. (A full narrative summary of Henry Ward, a case developed for training purposes, can be found in appendix B.)

Figure 5-2 shows a force-field analysis of Henry Ward. Some factors appear as complex forces, with aspects that both promote and resist law-abiding behavior. In Henry's case, the attachment to the mother is a driving force because it has potentially stabilizing effects, but her reciprocal behavior toward him makes it a restraining force as well. The force field includes as complete a list of driving forces as possible, because these are the strengths on which a supervision plan is built. This example simply presents a diagnostic technique; it does not pretend to offer the only or best way to interpret problems in a client. Several supervision methods could be deduced from this diagnostic instrument.

Certain patterns emerge from this force-field analysis. The most interdependent forces have to do with the mother's role: Henry now lives at home, and her influence reduces his willingness to face the meaning of his offense. A particularly strong force, however, is his unemployment, which also relates to a number of other forces, such as free time. Unemployment is a problem that can be changed rapidly, whereas other aspects of Henry's problems do not appear easily alterable: it is unlikely, for example, that supervision will dramatically increase his skill level. Thus, a brief analysis of forces indicates some candidate targets for change. Although all four forces have been listed here, in practice often only one or two key forces emerge. The person completing the force field should not feel compelled to over-

Forces **Driving** for More Law-Abiding Behavior	Forces **Restricting** Law-Abiding Behavior
1. Length of time since last serious offense (4 years) →	← 1. Very quick temper
2. Strong relationship with mother →	← 2. Previous inability to complete probation without violations
3. No serious mental or emotional problems →	← 3. Friends include persons who are marginally deviant
4. Has been able to find several jobs on his own →	← 4. Seriousness of current offense
5. Apparently wants to work as a truck driver →	← 5. Transient background
6. High to average intelligence →	6. Lack of male role model
7. School seems a possibility →	← 7. Immature behavior patterns
8. Newly developed relationship with H. Brown →	← 8. Lack of self-understanding
9. Apparently developing religious ties →	← 9. Poor school history
10. Apparent previous cooperative attitude on probation →	10. Mother apparently supports some antisocial behavior ←
11. Generally good physical health →	← 11. Sporadic work record
12. Girlfriend's parents' strong disapproval of the relationship →	← 12. Unwillingness to face the realities of his offense
	← 13. Expresses antisocial attitudes
	← 14. Occasional abuse of drugs and alcohol
	← 15. Presence of steady girlfriend
	← 16. Aimless use of free time

Figure 5-2. Force-Field Analysis of Probationer Henry Ward

select forces, since overselection may lead to overly intrusive supervision or lack of focus in the use of available resources.

Strength: relationship to mother, use of free time

Speed: unemployment

Alterability: unemployment, lack of male role model

Interdependence: unemployment, relationship to mother

Specification of Objectives

The third step in the case plan is the specification of supervision objectives. By stating outcomes, the supervision officer makes visible the level and extent of the intrusiveness of supervision. By stating outcomes that focus on a measurable criterion such as behavior, rather than on less-tangible offender characteristics such as attitudes, the supervision officer makes explicit the assumed links between supervision objectives and the dynamics of the case. Assumptions that appear to be unwarranted can then be questioned and revised. Finally, the focus on specificity makes it easier to test possible alternative approaches—to use less-intrusive objectives to achieve the same general risk-control end.

To obtain specific, measurable outcome statements, we needed a technique for recording case plans. We adapted one used by educators for several decades to achieve similar management purposes. The following discussion illustrates the importance of objectives setting in education and its adaptability to community supervision.

Behavioral Objectives in Education

Educators have used behavioral-outcome statements—also called behavioral objectives—for a variety of purposes. The concept first evolved in the early 1900s, when educators began calling for articulation of specific educational objectives for purposes of "scientific" curriculum design. This movement, exemplified by Franklin Bobbit's classic, *The Curriculum,* was founded on the belief that "human life consists in its performance of specific activities. Education . . . prepares definitely and adequately and for these specific activities."[6] In an excess of enthusiasm for categorization, these early reformers tried to generate lists of all the social abilities Americans needed to gain through exposure to school. Bobbit provided a comprehensive listing of over 160 objectives, ranging from "ability to protect home from fire" to "the mental, moral, and social qualities necessary for parenthood and proper character."[7] One of Bobbit's contemporaries listed 1,581 social objectives for English alone.[8] Eventually, as might be expected, this approach "collapsed under its own weight":[9]

> Teachers could not manage fifty highly specific objectives, let alone hundreds. And, in addition, the new view of the child, not as a complex

machine, but as a growing organism who ought to participate in planning his own education program, did not mesh well with the theoretical views held earlier.[10]

The failure of this movement has lessons for community supervision. The purpose of specifying objectives is not to compile a list of all possible supervision objectives or even a set of standard objectives that will somehow apply to all offenders. Rather, the goal is to develop officers' skills to compile a unique, useful set of objectives that reflects a view of each offender as a dynamic organism willing and able to participate in the supervision process.

The renewal of the objectives-specification movement in education, generally attributed to the influence of Ralph W. Tyler, focused on curriculum policy and planning. In an early essay, Tyler stated the four basic questions that must be answered in building a curriculum:

1. What educational purposes should the school seek to obtain?
2. What educational experiences can be provided that are likely to obtain these purposes?
3. How can these educational experiences be effectively organized?
4. How can we determine whether these purposes are being attained?[11]

These questions are remarkably similar to the kinds of questions relevant to community supervision and are related to the same kind of confusion over purposes, techniques, and effectiveness.

The renewed interest in specifying objectives in education has spawned a wide variety of innovation, including advanced learning theory,[12] taxonomies of educational outputs,[13] preparation of machine-aided instruction,[14] and even comprehensive curriculum design.[15] Literally hundreds of doctoral dissertations are still addressing the central role of objectives-specification in education.

This movement, too, has come under criticism. Elliot Eisner has pointed out that frequently

> teachers seem not to take educational objectives seriously. . . . Their efforts [to set objectives] appear to be more like exercises gone through than serious efforts to build tools for curricular planning. If educational objectives were really useful tools, teachers . . . would use them. If they do not, perhaps it is not because there is something wrong with the teachers, but because there might be something wrong with the theory.[16]

The tendency among teachers to resist specifying objectives raises a parallel concern for community supervision: how can objectives specification be kept a dynamic part of the supervision procedure rather than a meaningless paperwork exercise like so many other aspects of case recording? Insight into sources of resistance among teachers can provide lessons for community-supervision efforts. Miriam Kapfer contends that one reason for nonuse is the difficulty of creating teaching materials that incorporate the behavioral approach.[17] W. James Popham argues more bluntly that "teaching . . . at the moment just isn't good enough,"[18] and that their awareness of personal inadequacies leads many teachers to resist quantification of the results of their efforts.

Regardless of the criticisms, behavioral-objective specification and the controversies the method has created occupy a central position in contemporary education technology. Experience with objectives specification in education suggests that the method may have significance for community supervision in three areas: goal articulation, selection of interventions, and evaluation.

Goal Articulation

John Flanagan had said that "the huge advantage of an instructional objective derives from the simple fact that it is written. Once it is written, it is visible. Once it is visible, it can be reviewed, evaluated, modified, and improved."[19] This visibility of goals makes public debate (if not consensus) about their suitability possible and thus serves as the ultimate check on discretion. For educators, making specific objectives visible is a natural way of responding to questions regarding the purposes of public education: the purpose is change, and the changes can be defined as the important new behaviors produced as a result of the education process.

> It is far *easier* for educators to attend to *important* instructional outcomes. To illustrate, if you were to ask a social science teacher what his objectives were for his government class, and he responded as follows, "I want to make my students better citizens so that they can function effectively in our nation's dynamic democracy," you would probably find little reason to fault him. His objective sounds so profound and eminently worthwhile that few would criticize it. Yet, beneath such a facade of profundity, many teachers are aiming at extremely trivial kinds of pupil behavior changes. How often, for example, do we find "good citizenship" measured by a trifling true-false test? Now if we'd ask for the teacher's objectives in operational terms and discovered that indeed all the teacher was attempting to do was promote the learner's achievement on a true-false test, we might have rejected the aim as being unimportant. But this is possible *only* with the precision of explicitly stated goals.[20]

Similarly, stating that the objective of community supervision is to help the offender adjust (reintegrate, habilitate) into the community is not enough. Too often, the real requirements are regular reporting and a pretense of participation in an interaction that can be only loosely defined as counseling. Few would support such a short-sighted approach. Objectives specification forces the officer to confront the behavior-specific requirements of his work.

Objectives also help to clarify exactly what those goals should be. Often, service provision and surveillance are stated as the functions of supervision, but these terms invariably embrace a more concrete set of officer expectations of offender behavior. Making the value judgments of supervision officers explicit through behavioral objectives clarifies their relation (or lack of relation) to the larger goal of risk control.

Behavioral objectives also highlight the fact that the true substance of supervision is offender behavior and not offender attitudes. They make it possible to assign appropriate treatment for the offender who appears to have a good attitude but continues to engage in criminal behavior and for the offender who is crime free but appears to have a bad attitude.

Selection of Interventions

Kapfer has stated that

> behaviorally stated objectives are increasingly accepted as keys which unlock the doors of better instruction and more productive learning. They are tools which let students know where they are going so they will make intelligent choices how they will get there.[21]

This is a very simple concept: the formulation of specific objectives lets the teacher select the educational experiences likely to produce the objectives and allows students to orient their study and practice to those objectives.

Some observers have criticized this approach—which calls for formulating objectives first, then identifying classroom experiences designed to meet those objectives—on the grounds that it fails to take into account "the real world."[22] In reality, it is argued, "the teacher . . . asks a fundamentally different question from 'what am I trying to do?' The teacher asks 'what am I going to do?' and out of the doing comes the accomplishment."[23] The latter approach, whether due to laziness or caprice, is clearly insufficient in the context of community supervision, where there is already a tendency to provide the same kind of supervision interventions for everybody. Moreover, a growing body of research indicates that these shotgun-style approaches to handling offenders, such as individual counseling and group counseling, are not effective. A much more reasonable approach is to prescribe interventions specifically designed to achieve the unique objectives required for individual clients. This approach would be consistent with much contemporary research[24] and would help protect clients from actual harm as a result of inappropriate interventions.[25]

Specifying objectives before selecting interventions also eliminates idiosyncratic approaches to supervision. To the degree that the ambiguity surrounding the use of discretion in supervision allows officers to pursue their own favorite methods regardless of relevance to the case, requiring previous statements of outcomes will aid in identifying offenders for whom those favorite methods are inappropriate.

Evaluation

The most forceful and most convincing arguments in favor of behavioral objectives in education concern their role in evaluation. Originally it was believed that a finite set of objectives would form the basis for evaluating all schools. Later, objectives-setting was seen as a key element in developing the dynamic curricular program, whereby "the objectives of the school are clearly specified and the school system is evaluated and modified to maximize the extent to which these objectives are achieved.[26] A set of objectives also created the "additional advantage that the student is provided a means to evaluate *his own* progress at any place along the route of instruction; and is able to organize his efforts into relevant activities."[27]

That objectives specification has increased the evaluative capabilities of educational researchers is undeniable. The research questions asked and results obtained so far have addressed the effectiveness of objectives-based classrooms,[28] prior knowledge of objectives,[29] self-selected objectives,[30] and specificity of objectives.[31] None of this research nor any of the many other technique-comparative research efforts in education would have been possible without a developed technology of objectives-setting.

Objectives-setting could play a parallel role in evaluating specific probation interventions. Holding aside, for the moment, problems of random selection, chance apprehension, and so forth, the basic model is very simple: given the same objective for two groups of people but two different means (programs, services, activities) of achieving the result, which group has the higher proportion of successes? A whole array of collateral questions emerges: What is the effect of sharing versus not sharing the objective with the offender? What is the effect of offender agreement with the objective? What is the effect of offender participation in the selection of the objective? Are objectives independent, or does the achievement of one seem to influence the achievement of others? Does objectives-based supervision produce more successes than traditional supervision? And so on.

The specification of objectives makes this array of research activities available to the probation system. What Daniel Glaser refers to as "routinized evaluation"—continuing, systematic, program-based research as opposed to one-shot evaluative studies—is now a real possibility.[32]

Specifying Behavioral Objectives

Each of the several how-to-write-objectives manuals now available has its own prescription for writing high-quality objectives, but the differences are not as great as the similarities.[33] The book most widely recommended by the experts is Robert F. Mager's *Preparing Instructional Objectives* (also published as *Preparing Objectives for Programmed Instruction*). Mager's description of the technique is representative. He begins by defining the terminology of objectives:

> Behavior—refers to any visible activity displayed by a learner (student).
>
> Terminal Behavior—refers to the behavior you would like your learner to be able to demonstrate at the time your influence over him ends.
>
> Criterion—is a standard or test by which terminal behavior is evaluated.[34]

A behavioral objective is a stated outcome that uses "visible activity." It avoids ambiguous terminology.

> Though it is all right to include such words as "understand" and "appreciate" in a statement of an objective, the statement is not explicit enough to be useful until it indicates how you intend to sample the "understanding' and "appreciating." Until you describe what the user will be DOING when demonstrating that he "understands" or "appreciates," you have described very little at all. Thus, the statement which communicates best will be one which describes the terminal behavior of the learner well enough to preclude misinterpretation.[35]

Identification of the terminal behavior is the first of a three-step objective-declaration process:

> First, identify the terminal behavior by name; we can specify the kind of behavior which will be accepted as evidence that the learner has achieved the objective.
>
> Second, try to further define the desired behavior by describing the important conditions under which the behavior will be expected to occur.
>
> Third, specify the criteria of acceptable performance by describing how well the learner must perform to be considered acceptable.[36]

According to Mager, then, a "meaningful" objective has three components: terminal behavior, condition, and criterion. For example:

1. [Given a list of 35 chemical elements,] the learner must be able to
             condition

[recall and write the valences] [of at least 30.]
    terminal behavior   *criterion*

2. [Without the aid of a slide rule,]
          condition
the learner will be able to [calculate the square roots]
             terminal behavior
[of at least 20 out of 25 two-digit integers accurately to .0002 percent.]
            criterion

Ralph W. Tyler, the founder of the current rationalist movement in education, has questioned the validity of this emphasis on specificity:

> I think many current uses of the term, *behavioral objectives,* imply procedures that are too specific. I believe that the individual human being is able to solve many of his own problems and so I think that more of our educational objectives should be general in nature—like learning how to go about attacking problems, finding out where the difficulties are, getting information, analyzing the data, and drawing inferences from the data. Hence, in my view, many behavioral objectives should be set at a considerably higher and more general level than the extremely specific things I find in many current efforts to write them.[37]

Educators have recognized, for example, that some experiences have justifiable value despite a general inability to specify outcome objectives for them, concert such as attending a concern of classical music. Learning objectives related to these activities are unpredictable and highly individualized, yet the activities have value for the curriculum. Thomas S. Nagel and Paul T. Richmond have coined the term *expressive objectives* for these experientially based objectives.[38]

Determining the appropriate degree of specificity is equally difficult in community supervision. Should the very precise standards of Mager and others be followed? Or is there greater wisdom in maintaining some generality, as Tyler suggests? For example, allowing more general statements may help prevent the requirement of trivial activities merely to satisfy the technical requirements of a written objective. In addition, it is difficult to see precisely what form conditions can take in a written supervision objective, since the performances occur not in the controlled environment of the classroom, but in real life. It makes little sense, for example, to try to include conditions and a criterion for the objective "to discontinue use of heroin." On the other hand, "absent an excuse accepted by the probation officer, the probationer will not be more than fifteen minutes late to any office visits for the next six-month reporting period" includes all three of

Mager's characteristics and is a more useful objective because it does. Given the nature of probation supervision, the most reasonable requirement may be for the probation officer to write the objective as specifically as possible, but to at least state the exact behaviors being expected of the probationers.

There may also be occasions when the probation officer needs to write an expressive objective. For example, the officer may want the client to undergo professional diagnosis, even though the behavioral goals (following the diagnosis) may be largely unpredictable. In these circumstances, an objective such as "to attend Kellog Psychiatric Center for diagnosis one hour a week until a full diagnosis is completed" might be acceptable. However, because expressive objectives represent interventions that often have unclear outcomes and are therefore difficult to justify under existing risk-control norms, they should be avoided whenever possible.

The overriding consideration is to write objectives that will be useful for guiding the officer's supervision decisions, for reviewing the basis for discretionary decisions, and for evaluating the effectiveness of supervision methods aimed at achieving change. Five guidelines provide a key to writing useful objectives.

1. *The objective should describe behavior.* The most common failing of written objectives is that they do not describe the behavioral referent. For example, the attitudinal goal "to increase self-confidence" does not contain a behavioral referent. When the change goal for a client is primarily attitudinal, in order to set a behavioral objective, the supervision officer must ask what behavior can serve as an indicator that the attitude change has occurred. If the supervision officer is working on self-confidence in order to help the client look for employment, for example, the behavioral objective may to "to look for employment by visiting at least one potential employer a day until a job is found," since self-confidence would be involved in the achievement of the change.

2. *The behavior described should be that of the client, not of the agency.* Another common error is to state the goals of the caseworker rather than those of the client. For example, "to help the probationer learn to read at current grade level by the end of the school year" is a behavioral objective for the officer, not for the client. When all references to the caseworker's activities are eliminated, the objective becomes "to learn to read at current grade level by the end of the school year."

3. *The behavior should be as specific as possible.* The more specific an objective, the easier it is for the probation officer to know when it has been achieved, and for the offender to understand his or her responsibilities. Although it may be impossible to be completely specific, the client's objective should be stated as specifically as possible. For example, "to get a job" can be changed into "to obtain full-time employment as an auto mechanic within three months."

4. *The objective should describe an outcome, not a technique.* Another common error in setting objectives is to include the technique in the statement of the objective. A true objective describes only a goal. If it is specific enough, it will aid in decision making about techniques for achieving that goal, but it should not include the technique in the goal statement itself. For example, the objective "to give client and wife counseling about their relationship" is a statement that confuses the supervision technique and supervision goal. "To reduce amount of fighting with wife over the next three months" would be a clearer objective. The resource (or technique) of counseling by the probation officer can be listed separately as related to that goal, and its effectiveness as a technique evaluated later.

5. *A case should not contain too many behavioral objectives.* Sometimes the supervision officer feels that something has been left out of a case once the objectives have been stated and responds by writing more objectives. It is important to remember that a single objective such as "to attend school this term without absences" may require a major change in the client's life (and a great deal of work by the supervision officer). To overload a client with objectives would be to set unrealistic goals.

In experimenting with methods for writing objectives, we found a simple, three-part model the most useful in guiding officers to write good behavioral objectives: Starting with the word *to* puts the statement in a forward-looking, hence objective, format. The behavioral goal, the client's target behavior for change, follows. Last comes the criterion, which stipulates a time period in which the objective's behavior will be exhibited or a level of achievement required. The following list contains some typical objectives.

To continue to be employed full-time at Harper's Food Mart while on probation

To obtain full-time employment during the day within one month

To complete a job-training program by the end of the calendar year

To complete a high-school-equivalency program and receive a diploma

To discontinue all use of narcotic drugs while on probation

To limit drinking to no more than two beers per weekday, four per day on weekends

To spend no time with codefendent while on probation

To make at least two new friends with boys of own age in the next six weeks

Table 5-4 shows some common errors made in writing objectives. It also demonstrates how they might be corrected.

Table 5-4
Sample Incorrect and Correct Versions of Written Objectives

Incorrect	*Correct*
Nonbehavioral	*Behavioral*
To improve relationship with wife	To stop all physical fighting with wife while on probation
To develop self-control	To be at home by 10 p.m. on workdays
To accept responsibility for behavior	To earn money to pay victim for all automobile damages within three months
Non-Client-related	*Client-related*
To get probationer to stop stealing from mother	To stop taking money from mother without permission
To help probationer finish school (not get expelled)	To obtain high-school equivalency from adult-education program within six months
To motivate probationer to discuss problems with parents	To discuss problems with parents whenever they are causing you concerns
Nonspecific	*More Specific*
To go to school	To attend school regularly with no unexcused absences each month
To avoid bad companions	To terminate all relationships with "Eagle" gang members while on probation
To improve school performance	To receive no grades below C this term
To get probationer to develop inner controls	To stop fighting with next-door neighbor while on probation
To related better to probation officer	To discuss daily activities openly with probation officer when asked
To have probationer attend mental-health clinic	To make and attend regular appointments at the mental-health clinic until diagnosis is completed

In the example of Henry Ward discussed earlier, a force-field analysis identified four key forces:

1. Unemployment
2. Use of free time
3. Relationship to mother
4. Lack of male role model

These four forces could be translated into the following behavioral objectives:

1. To obtain full-time employment and stay employed during supervision period (critical)

2. To attend night school at least two nights a week taking courses of his own choice (somewhat important)
3. To move out of mother's home into a residence approved by probation officer within six months (very important)
4. To continue to meet with Father Brown at least once a week for the next four months (somewhat important)

In this case, a behavioral objective has been written in response to each key force. In other cases, a force may require more than one objective, or some key forces may be ignored in order to avoid overloading the case with objectives.

The final step in objectives specification is to rate the importance of each objective, as in the parenthetical terms after each objective above. Differentiating the risk-control potential of each objective provides a basis for more relevant evaluation of supervision discretion. Objectives can be rated as critical, very important, somewhat important, or of little importance. The last category should be used infrequently.

Specification of Resources

The final step in the case analysis is to list the resources to be used to achieve each specified objective. Listing specific resources rather than general functions or activities helps decision makers to evaluate the utility of those resources for achieving the objectives. Therefore, "Merton Mental Health Clinic" would be used instead of the more-general "individual counseling." If more than one resource is related to an objective, one can be classified as primary and the other as secondary. If the same resource is related to several objectives, it can be listed separately for each. Later, evaluation may reveal that a particular community agency is effective in helping clients meet only some of the objectives for which it is frequently used.

Very often, the probation officer (or the general-supervision process) will constitute the major resource for achieving the objective. In that case, the officer can specify the resource as "individual counseling by probation officer" or simply "probation officer." Officers who believe in allowing the client as much responsibility as possible for the change effort might think of the client as the resource for some objectives. Given that the resource-articulation phase permits subsequent evaluation of the methods of intervention, the method should be specified. In a nondirective approach, the resource is really the supervision relationship between the officer and client. Therefore, what should be evaluated in this instance is the officer's choice of technique, and the resource should be listed as the supervision officer.

For future needs assessment, it is helpful to have an initial subjective rating of the perceived capacity of the resource to achieve the specific objective. The officer may rate the resource as excellent, good, fair, or poor, bearing in mind that the rating reflects only a perception of probable utility for a particular objective. Thus, the supervising officer may feel that the resource (perhaps his or her own counseling skill) is generally of high quality but is ill suited to achieve a particularly difficult or complicated objective. Table 5-5 lists specific resources to be used for each of Henry Ward's objectives.

Using the Case Plan

So far, we have presented guidelines useful in the formulation of an objectives-based diagnostic and planning instrument. It remains to demonstrate how the case plan can serve as the officer's guide to evaluating and conducting the supervision activity while it is occurring.

Three methods can help ensure that the plan is dynamic and meaningful. The first is to include a narrative summary—the common method of recording case observations, contacts, and other pertinent chronological data about supervision—with the supervision plan.

Table 5-5
Objectives and Resources for Henry Ward

Objective	Importance of Objective	Resource	Rating of Resource
To obtain full-time employment and stay employed during supervision period	Critical	Lake City Employment Agency	Poor
To attend night school at least two nights a week, taking courses of his own choice	Somewhat important	Central High School	Good
To move out of mother's home into a residence approved by probation officer within six months	Very important	Counseling by probation officer	Fair
To continue to meet with Chaplain Brown at least once a week for the next four months	Somewhat important	H. Brown	Excellent

The second method is to conduct a regular (perhaps semiannual) evaluation of the offender's performance on the objectives, ranging from completed, through good, fair, and poor progress, to no longer applicable if an objective was later determined by the officer and client or supervisor to be inappropriate. This is also a time to add new objectives that may have become appropriate. This progress rating completes the information loop and provides the basis for feedback on supervision effectiveness: What objectives tend to be achieved? What objectives are related to recidivism in achievement/nonachievement? The progress report can also serve as the basis for deciding when to terminate supervision of the case.

The third method is perhaps the most important to involve both the client and the officer's supervisor in the case-planning process. The client hopefully is involved in constructing the case plan in order to increase his or her understanding of and commitment to the objectives of supervision. Some of the officers we worked with planned supervision with their clients beginning with a jointly constructed force-field and ending with an objectives contract.

The client should also be involved because risk-control values suggest that the client have some say in the objectives for which he or she is held responsible. For example, because Henry Ward is a level-2 client, the supervision objectives set for him (primarily objectives 2 and 4) are essentially voluntary and should not be established without his consent. Risk-control objectives reflecting incapacitatives aims, however (such as objectives 1 and 3), are more central to his law-abiding functioning and can be established by the officer as required controls on behavior.

The supervisor plays a key role in the process of sorting out supervision intentions by systematically reviewing and approving of all case plans prior to implementation. In this way the supervisor takes responsibility for the appropriateness of the interventions by line staff in supervising clients. This part of the supervisor's role is discussed in detail in the next chapter.

Testing the Risk-Control Model

We developed the objectives-based case-planning approach in our work with a team of probation officers in a large eastern metropolitan city (Big City). The final model was packaged into a training document called the Program Plan Profile (see appendix A). To test the utility of this approach, we trained probation officers in two other eastern agencies to do objectives-based case planning—Eastern Suburbs and Lake City Family Court (a juvenile-probation agency). The model translated extremely well into these new areas, and we gathered additional data from all three agencies to advance our understanding of it. These data included:

1. *"Live" cases:* Case plans prepared in accordance with the Program Plan Profile for actual cases under supervision
2. *"Standard" cases:* Risk-control analysis based on narrative information from presentence investigations, for five cases adapted from existing case files
3. *Attitudinal data:* A series of standardized attitudinal questionnaires administered to the officers who completed the standard cases
4. *Interview data:* Interviews of 85 probationers on their reaction to the objectives their officers had written for them

The characteristics of the three agencies and the amount of data they furnished are listed below.

Big-City Probation Department: This agency handles adult misdemeanants, many of whom have committed felonies that were plea bargained down to misdemeanors. Many of the clients come from the surrounding ghetto neighborhood and have extensive records. Over a fifteen-month period, 231 new cases were recorded and updated with risk-control model. In addition, twenty-one officers completed the five standard cases and the attitudinal questionnaires.

Eastern-Suburbs Probation Department: Over a three-month period, this combination of five suburban misdemeanant and juvenile courts used the PPP to analyze 190 cases (about 4 percent of the population) selected nonrandomly by twenty-five supervising officers and to conduct 85 interviews of probationers.

Lake City Family Court: Nineteen officers in this juvenile-probation agency analyzed the standard cases and completed the attitudinal questionnaires.

In addition to quantitative data, the staff of these three agencies in numerous formal and informal meetings provided invaluable qualitative insights into the concepts of risk control and the process of objectives-specification.[39] The data form the basis for our discussions of community supervision in part III.[40]

Notes

1. Marvin Bornstedt et al., *Classification for Field Services* (Washington, D.C.: National Institute of Corrections, 1980).
2. Compare General Accounting Office, *State and County Probation Systems Need to Be Better Managed* (Washington, D.C.: Government Print-

ing Office, 1977); and Kevin Wright and Paul Dickson, "Validation of the Wisconsin Risk Screening Model on New York City Probationers," mimeographed (Department of Probation, New York City, 1981).

3. Stephen Gottfredson and Don M. Gottfredson, "Screening for Risk: A Comparison of Methods," *Criminal Justice and Behavior* 8 (1981):1-21.

4. For discussion of the relation between a client's employment and the success of supervision, see David T. Stanley, *Prisoners among Us: The Problem of Parole* (Washington, D.C.: Brookings Institution, 1976); for the influence of financial support, see Kenneth Lenihan, "Financial Aid for Released Prisoners: An Experiment in Reducing Recidivism" (Paper presented at the meeting of the American Society of Criminology, Atlanta, November 1977).

5. Kurt Lewin, *Field Theory in Social Science* (New York: Harper & Row, 1951).

6. Franklin Bobbit, *The Curriculum* (Boston: Houghton Mifflin, 1918), p. 42.

7. Ibid., p. 211.

8. Elliot Eisner, "Educational Objectives: Help or Hindrance?" *School Review* 75 (1967):255.

9. Ibid.

10. Ibid., p. 256.

11. Ralph W. Tyler, *Basic Principles of Curriculum and Instruction* (Chicago: University of Chicago Press, 1950), pp. 1-2.

12. Robert M. Gagne, *The Conditions of Learning* (New York: Holt, Rinehart and Winston, 1965).

13. See Benjamin S. Bloom, ed., *Taxonomy of Educational Objectives, Handbook I: Cognitive Domain* (New York: David McKay, 1956); and David R. Krathwohl, Benjamin S. Bloom, and Bertram Masia, *Taxonomy of Educational Objectives, Handbook II: Affective Domain* (New York: David McKay, 1964).

14. See Charles S. Morrel, "Setting Programmed Instruction Objectives Using Systems Methodology," in *Trends in Programmed Instruction*, W.C. Muerhenery, ed. (Washington, D.C.: National Education Association, 1964), p. 51.

15. David A. Abrahamson, "Curriculum Research and Evaluation," *Review of Educational Research* 36 (1966):388.

16. Eisner, "Educational Objectives," p. 258.

17. Miriam B. Kapfer, ed., *Behavioral Objectives in Curriculum Development: Selected Readings and Bibliography* (Englewood Cliffs, N.J.: Educational Technology Publications, 1971), p. vii.

18. W. James Popham, "Probing the Validity of Arguments against Behavioral Goals," in Kapfer, *Behavioral Objectives in Curriculum Development*, p. 394.

19. John C. Flanagan, William M. Shanner, and Robert F. Mager,

Social Studies Behavioral Objectives (Palo Alto, Calif.: Westinghouse Learning Press, 1971), p. v.

20. Popham, "Probing Arguments against Behavioral Goals," p. 393.

21. Kapfer, *Behavioral Objectives in Curriculum Development*, p. vii.

22. Susan M. Markle and Philip W. Tremann, "Behavioral Analysis of Cognitive Content," *Educational Technology* 10 (1970):41.

23. James B. MacDonald, "Myths about Instruction," *Educational Leadership* 22 (1965):613-614.

24. Marguerite Q. Warren, "All Things Being Equal . . . ," *Criminal Law Bulletin* 9 (1973):483.

25. Stuart Adams, "Effectiveness of Interview Therapy with Older Youth Authority Wards: An Interim Evaluation of the PICO Project," mimeographed (California Youth Authority, Sacramento, 1961).

26. Harry F. Silberman and Laura F. Carter, "The Systems Approach, Technology and the School," in *New Approaches to Individualizing Instruction* (Princeton: Educational Testing Service, 1972), pp. 71-72.

27. Robert F. Mager, *Preparing Objectives for Programmed Instruction* (Palo Alto, Calif.: Fearon Press, 1962), p. 4.

28. See James Victor McCullouch, "The Effect of Using a Behavioral-Objectives Curriculum in Mathematics on the Achievement of Ninth-Grade Pupils in the Meridian Separate School District" (Ph.D. diss., University of Alabama, School of Education, 1970); and Robert Glaser and James H. Reynolds, "Instructional Objectives and Programmed Instruction: A Case Study," in *Defining Education Objectives: A Report to the Regional Commission on Educational Coordination and the Learning Research and Development Center*, ed. Lindyall (Pittsburgh: University of Pittsburgh Press, 1964), p. 47.

29. See Carlton Herman Stedman, "The Effects of Prior Knowledge of Behavioral Objectives on Cognitive Learning Outcomes Using Programmed Materials in Genetics" (Ph.D. diss., Indiana University, School of Education, 1970); Dorris Elaine Boardman, "The Effects of Students' Advanced Knowledge of Behavioral Objectives on Their Achievement in Remedial Chemistry" (Ph.D. diss., University of California at Los Angeles, School of Education 1970); and Charles Moorehouse Bidwell, "The Effect of Prior Knowledge of Instructional Objectives on Student Responses to Lecture Content and Presentation" (Ph.D. diss., Syracuse University, School of Education, 1971).

30. Bruce Donald Burr, "Student Participation in the Selection of Instructional Objectives for a Computer Resource Guide Which Teaches Us to Preplan the Individualization of Instruction" (Ph.D. diss., State University of New York at Buffalo, School of Education, 1971); and Gordon Peter Bianchi, "A Descriptive Comparison of the Differences among Instructional Objectives Which Are Formulated and Selected With and Without the

Participation of Students" (Ph.D. diss., State University of New York at Buffalo, School of Education, 1970).

31. Gus Thomas Dalis, "The Effect of Precise Objectives on Student Achievement in Health Education" (Ph.D. diss. University of California at Los Angeles, School of Education, 1969).

32. Daniel Glaser, *Routinizing Evaluation: Getting Feedback on the Effectiveness of Crime and Delinquency Programs* (Washington, D.C.: National Institute of Mental Health, Center for Studies of Crime and Delinquency, 1973).'

33. See Thomas S. Nagel and Paul T. Richman, *Competency-based Instruction: A Strategy to Eliminate Failure* (Columbus: Charles S. Merrill, 1972); David E. Hernandez, *Writing Behavioral Objectives: A Programmed Exercise for Beginners* (New York: Barnes and Noble, 1971); Thorwald Esbensen, "Writing Instructional Objectives," *Phi Delta Kappan*, 48 (January 1967):246-247; and Stuart R. Johnson and Rita B. Johnson, *Developing Individualized Instructional Material* (Palo Alto, Calif.: Westinghouse Learning Press, 1970).

34. Mager, *Preparing Objectives for Programmed Instruction*, p. 2.

35. Ibid., p. 11.

36. Ibid., p. 12.

37. "Ralph Tyler Discusses Behavioral Objectives," interview in *Today's Education: Journal of the National Education Association* 62 (September-October 1973):42. Reprinted with permission.

38. Nagel and Richman, *Competency-based Instruction*, p. 26.

39. The data were collected in a series of externally funded projects. Final reports of these projects are: Vincent O'Leary and Todd R. Clear, "Team Supervision in Probation" (Report to the National Science Foundation, Washington, D.C., 1973); Vincent O'Leary, Todd R. Clear, and James Fox, "Final Report: Middlesex Country Probation Needs Assessment" (Report to the Middlesex County Probation Services, Albany, 1974); and Training Center, National Council on Crime and Delinquency, "Team Supervision in Probation" (Report to the Monroe County Juvenile Court, 1973).

40. A handful of cases eminently due for termination were not transferred to the objectives-based information model because the officers believed it not worth the trouble.

Part III
Management of Risk Control

6

The Function of
Line Management

The two major ideas developed so far are, first, that the conceptual basis for community supervision is risk control, and that the nature and degree of supervision ought to reflect legitimate risk-control aims; and, second, that the dynamics of the work world of community-supervision personnel suggest the need for a structured approach to case classification and planning. In developing the objectives-based case plan, we have assumed that there is a natural connection between the elements of a result-oriented plan written in the supervision office and the larger purpose of risk control.

In principle, the amount of control exercised over an offender—the degree of intrusiveness into his life—no matter how beneficient the intent, must be limited in its intensity and scope to that appropriate to the punishment deserved and the risk posed by the offender. Intensity is largely regulated, in the system we envision, by the scales and related program categories we discussed in chapter 3. Scope is monitored through the behavioral-objectives scheme described in chapter 5, in which a limited number of objectives are stated openly and subject to review by a third party.

Objectives may serve the purposes of desert, as in the case of restitution payments imposed by a court or risk-control goals as, for example, when an offender is required to attend a drug-rehabilitation program. It is the latter type of objectives with which we will be largely engaged here, but it is well to emphasize that our model, after all, is labeled *constrained risk control* and there is a continuing concern with appropriate and proportionate punishments, as well as the suppression of crime.

Yet it is one thing to establish a conceptual system and describe its implications for community supervision, and quite another to *implement it* in day-to-day work. Here is where the practical test of any criminal-justice change effort occurs. In our effort to achieve real change, organic change, in the work of community supervision, rather than simply requiring new paperwork, we sought to alter the approaches community-supervision workers adopted and to focus their decisions on the objective of constrained risk control.

We learned that if risk-control-oriented supervision was to become a routine reality, the role of the supervision office had to change in at least three ways. First, office workers could no longer operate in isolation. Isolation reinforces idiosyncratic work styles, and developing a sense of interdependence among workers is a first step toward structured risk-control supervision. Second, we had to create a climate in which officers could view their work critically. This meant that we had to establish feedback mechanisms that were accurate and comfortable, challenging without being threatening. Third, we had to redefine the role of the unit supervisor as a more managerial one; the unit supervisor would have to make resource-allocation decisions and hold line officers accountable for their work.

In short, we had to change the role of the supervision unit from its traditional one of serving primarily as a tool of administrative convenience to one in which it would serve as the basic operational tool of the supervision workforce. In this new role, the supervision unit would critically assess and resolve the central problems of supervision policy. Rather than viewing caseloads as the core organizing principle of supervision, we had to redefine office routines so as to increase the significance of the supervision unit as the line organizational mechanism. This task was necessary because we saw the community-supervision office as a system in which the technical and human aspects of the office are mutually reinforcing components of supervision practice. So long as officers are isolated from one another and technologically alienated from their immediate unit manager, systematic, controlled supervision is impossible. So long as supervision officers rely primarily on individualized and unobtrusive discretion, structured and focused risk-control supervision will occur only as a result of the choice of individual officers. We recognized that, to be successful, we must focus as much on the attitudes of the office as on the techniques of the officers.

The result was a carefully designed collaborative effort in which researchers and staff worked together to develop supervision technologies. The initial steps and product of this process—the objectives-based case plan—have already been described in part II. Once it was designed, this instrument for documenting risk control helped us study and alter the supervision methods of the units we worked with. In fact most of the project was spent learning how to use objectives-based information to improve the supervision process.

Our aim was organic change, in which the workers themselves would design, criticize, and revise their own tools and methods of supervision. If the new tools implemented were not seen as credible and useful, they would never replace previous approaches to which staff had developed personal commitments.[1]

It was not an altogether amicable process. As in most human-service agencies, the supervision staff with whom we worked were suspicious of the motives of outside researchers and skeptical about administrative agenda for change. Large workloads helped to reinforce a belief that it was nearly impossible to influence work positively. Interpersonal strains often affected the tone of meetings and discussions. Thus, most of the typical obstacles to change were present. Nevertheless, our commitment to organic change allowed us to overcome most of these obstacles, and the staff maintained an often-surprising level of excitement for the research tasks as well as the technical tasks. In retrospect, we can identify three elements that are fundamental to success in an organic-change effort.

1. *Managerial support must be visibly present.* Without visible and unequivocal support from management, staff are likely to expect that the changes or suggestions they make will be ignored at higher organizational levels. The top administrator must support both the aims and process of organic change and allow the collaborative team substantial autonomy and discretion. This can be accomplished simply by having the top leadership attend the initial meetings of the project team and give them an unofficial mandate.

While permission from the very top is important, active support from the line units' "boundary keepers"—the supervisor and his/her immediate superior—is crucial to success, since the work of the group is likely to threaten their previous roles and activities. It is important to involve these people at virtually every stage of the change process, keeping their support active and apparent.

2. *Premature solutions must be avoided.* Organic change requires that the form and details of the change itself emerge from the people whose attitudes and practices must be altered. People learn by discussion, criticism, and problem solving. Even problems that are apparently easily resolved must receive full consideration, for while the surface issue may have an obvious answer, the underlying problems of project rationale and task commitment can be addressed only through free and open interchange. Participants are likely to question solutions adopted too quickly because they have forgotten the original reasons for the solution.

Thus, we consistently brought virtually every issue to our teams for their discussion. No problem was seen as too small or too explosive to be discussed. As a result, researchers and staff assumed collective responsibility for the direction of the project.

3. *Trust is crucial.* Organic-change efforts require people to assess critically their own styles and approaches to their work, and to do so in the presence of their peers. It is difficult to think of a more potentially threatening responsibility. Without a basic belief that the process will result in positive changes rather than punitive reactions, people will be unwilling to voice their basic concerns about needed innovation and will be hesitant to take risks.

Consequently, there must be a conscious effort to develop trust, to demonstrate that staff will not be adversely affected by fully participating in the project. All comments are considered potentially important, and decisions are not made without general group agreement. One reason for avoiding premature solutions is that later decisions to reject them reduces trust.

To guarantee the continuing operation of these three guiding principles, we emphasized the importance of meetings for discussion of project steps. In the process, we learned that feedback to staff is a powerful research and action tool.

Using Feedback to Develop Unit Competence

After the objectives-based case plan had been developed and tested, we began systematically to feed back to staff the aggregated results of the plans. Once data were available on current work with cases, our discussions of supervision methods focused on the actual material our officers had provided in their case plans.

The first feedback given to officers involved simply listing all the behavioral objectives each had developed for five cases in their existing caseload. It was a powerful experience as officers for the first time had the opportunity to see collectively the characteristics of a group of cases they were supervising. They were able to identify common problems that existed across caseloads, an ability that led to a growing awareness of the nature of the supervision process and of the new type of structures that would be needed to accomplish the tasks facing them. It did not take long, for example, for one officer to raise a question of whether their unit should continue to be organized in terms of caseloads or whether it would be better that certain officers be assigned to deal with certain classes of objectives. Thus one officer who had a particular skill in job development might deal with the employment needs of offenders, irrespective of the caseload to which they might be assigned currently. Officers also became more analytic and detached about their work. Thus, the group asked to see objectives broken down by individual officers, and when these data were presented to them, they asked why the patterns revealed existed. In short, the probation officers took on the role of researchers who worked in a collaborative mode with the outside consultants.

Questions of the following type were asked: What do officers *do* in the supervision of cases? How intrusive is the supervision effort? What risk-control methods does supervision entail? To answer these questions, we turned to the case plans. Since each supervision objective represents an intervention, we began by assessing the objectives themselves.

One of the most productive and least threatening methods of assessment was the aggregation of data into tables. Because variations in data illustrate the importance of variations in risk-control methods between organizations, when possible we compiled results from more than one project. Using these tables for feedback purposes frees supervision units to explore critically the way they do their work.

To help address one fundamental issue—whether behavioral objectives in community supervision are overly intrusive—we compiled a table showing the frequency of objectives of any type for cases in Big City and Eastern Suburbs (see table 6-1). This table indicates that, although individual cases may have had overly lenient or severe supervision approaches, there was no extreme pattern. Even when court conditions were added in, slightly less than 15 percent of the cases had more than four separate outcome goals specified.[2] In well over half of the cases, three or fewer outcome objectives were identified. The data indicate neither widespread meddling in clients' lives nor ineffective requirements. Over 80 percent of the cases had multiple-outcome requirements; when court conditions are included, this figure increases to over 90 percent. The frequency of objectives in the two agencies is very similar.

When we began to consider the types of objectives officers wrote, the requirement that officers specify unique objectives for each individual created problems for feedback. A set of unique objectives, not precoded, is difficult to aggregate, enumerate, and study. Technically, we would have been justified in compiling only objectives that were worded identically. However, to maintain a vast number of different, sometimes unique, objectives would make them virtually useless for systematic planning and policy-making.[3] As a result, we suppressed some of the information contained in specific objectives in order to group them for purposes of team discussion. In essence, we simply reversed the common approach to categorizing objectives.

Table 6-1
Distribution of Cases, by Number of Objectives: Big City and Eastern Suburbs

Number of Objectives	Big City		Eastern Suburbs	
	Number of Cases	Cumulative Frequency (percentage)	Number of Cases	Cumulative Frequency (percentage)
1	32	15.2	33	18.9
2	73	46.8	55	47.9
3	51	68.6	60	79.5
4	42	87.0	23	91.6
5	19	95.2	10	96.8
6	8	98.7	2	97.9
7	2	99.6	4	100.0
8	1	100.0	0	100.0
Total	231	100.0	190	100.0

Note: Kolmogorov-Smirnow two-sample test to establish that samples were drawn from different populations is not significant at .10 level; $D = -.107$.

Note: Three Big City cases (1.3 percent) and three Eastern Suburbs cases (1.6 percent) had no supervision objectives.

Table 6-2
Descriptive Categorization of Objectives: Big City and Eastern Suburbs

Descriptive Category of Objective	Big City		Eastern Suburbs	
	Number of Cases	Percentage of Cases	Number of Cases	Percentage of Cases
Get a new job	72	31.2	71	37.4
Maintain current employment	84	36.4	10	5.3
Improve employment through better job or training	45	19.5	37	19.5
Report regularly and on time	67	29.0	9	4.7
Return to or finish school; improve school behavior	43	18.6	31	16.3
Reduce or curtail drug usage	36	15.6	26	13.7
Improve relationship with certain persons	20	8.7	42	22.1
Modify drinking habits	14	6.1	31	16.3
Talk honestly and openly with probation officer	31	13.4	12	6.3
Use free time more constructively; avoid certain places; keep curfew; develop recreation interests	22	9.5	18	9.5
Enter or stay in drug or alcohol program	21	9.1	15	7.9
Curtail certain illegal activities (such as possession of handgun)	22	9.5	9	4.7
Terminate association with certain persons	22	9.5	8	4.2
Assume a specific financial responsibility: support; restitution	17	7.4	13	6.8
Get a new and stable place to live	14	6.1	16	8.4
Deal with emotional problems; gain maturity and insight	10	4.3	19	10.0
Get psychotherapeutic counseling	9	3.9	19	10.0
Set life goals/make certain life decisions	19	8.2	8	4.2
Accept referral to services of another specific agency	17	7.4	9	4.7
Make new friends	13	5.6	11	5.8
Accept authority of parent; court; probation officer	3	1.3	20	10.5
Attend group-counseling sessions	11	4.8	10	5.3
Get high-school-equivalency diploma	17	7.4	3	1.6
Become more assertive: improve self-image/self-confidence	3	1.3	17	8.9
Control anger/temper/aggressiveness	11	4.8	8	4.2
Improve financial situation; budget money	9	3.9	6	3.2
Get family counseling	3	1.3	11	5.8
Learn to read or write English	7	3.0	4	2.1
Get medical assistance: take medication	1	0.4	7	3.7
Accept residential placement	1	0.4	3	1.6
Live at home with parent or guardian	1	0.4	1	0.5

Note: $r_s = .260; p = > .05$

For example, the objectives "to maintain steady employment as a plumber" and "to continue to work at the factory" plausibly belong together under a descriptive heading "to maintain current employment." Similarly, both of these objectives could be differentiated from another descriptive group, "to obtain full-time employment." The result is that a category contains objectives of varying content, except for the behavior. Thus, the category "terminate certain relationships" might include such disparate objectives as "end gang membership immediately," "stop spending time with girlfriend," and "stay away from ex-wife during probation period."[4]

It would have been relatively easy to provide a set of standard objectives from which officers might select those appropriate to a given case. But it was and continues to be our belief that the dangers in such an approach were the loss of important information about individual cases and the likelihood of the routinization of the process. In our view, it was important for officers to go through the steps of articulating specific objectives for each case to preserve their unique character and reduce the danger of simply choosing from among previously established objectives that might have little to do with the reality of the supervision activity. While a standardized category of objectives emerged in each agency in which we worked, we maintained the original process for developing objectives. When required for analytic or administrative purposes, it was easy enough to code according to a standard set of objectives so that they could be aggregated for various purposes and treated statistically.

During the initial project, thirty-one descriptive categories were established for Big City cases. These categories were later applied to the Eastern Suburbs data. Table 6-2 lists the frequency distribution of cases having at least one objective of each type. The table illustrates the remarkable variety of risk-control interventions specified for cases. Only a handful of objectives appeared in more than 10 percent of the cases, and only one objective appeared in more than one-third of the cases in either sample. There are also several substantial differences between the samples in the frequency of objectives.

The data indicate that behavioral objectives as a supervision technology apparently did not lead to extensive intrusiveness. Three-fourths of the objectives would frequently relate closely to client desires (such as "get a job") or are minimally intrusive (such as "set life goals") or may well be required under any punishment-oriented system (reporting). This finding should not minimize the potential intrusiveness of particular objectives in individual cases; the tremendous variability in the officers' approaches to supervising cases was a central aspect of discussions during regular feedback sessions.

The large number of objective groupings and wide range of frequencies proved unwieldy for much of our work. Although the descriptive objectives were useful in discussing risk-control approaches to cases, the Big City probation officers suggested reducing the number of categories to investigate the aggregate supervision workload. They devised a functional-categorization method that reduced objectives to five groups.

Employment: related to obtaining, maintaining, or improving jobs

Education: related to formal schooling

Social: related to changes in patterns of interaction with other people

Health: related primarily to emotional adjustment of the offender, but also including medical-emotional areas such as drug and alcohol dependencies

Control: related to behavioral limitations of supervision (such as restricted mobility in living arrangements) that are applied for purposes of exerting authority over the client

Table 6-3 presents the distribution of functional objectives for both the Big City and Eastern Suburbs. The differences between the two samples may reflect some differences in environment and clientele. Big City's heavy reliance on employment objectives is consistent with the inner-city, urbanized, largely impoverished setting of the agency. Other differences, however, are more difficult to explain. The more extensive use of health objectives by Eastern Suburbs may indicate a tendency among officers there to accord more importance to emotionally based problem areas. While working with Eastern Suburbs officers, we perceived a greater willingness to use a medical-model approach, and their greater use of health-oriented objectives

Table 6-3
Distribution of Objectives, by Functional Category: Big City and Eastern Suburbs

Functional Category	Number of Objectives		Percentage of Objectives		Percentage of Cases with at Least One Objective		Percentage of Cases with Two or More Objectives in One Area	
	Big City	Eastern Suburbs	Big City	Eastern Suburbs	Big City	Eastern Suburbs	Big City	Eastern Suburbs
Employment	201	118	30.2	23.3	78.9	55.8	8.2	6.3
Education	122	126	18.3	24.9	39.0	50.0	.0	.0
Social	67	38	10.2	7.5	29.0	20.0	11.7	14.2
Health	115	139	17.3	27.5	40.3	55.3	8.7	13.7
Control	159	84	23.9	16.7	50.6	36.3	16.4	7.3
Total	664	505	100.0	100.0	—	—	—	—

(which reflect medical-model values) is consistent with that impression. Differences in the frequency of control objectives may reflect the fact that the disorganized nature of the Big City neighborhood made frequent home visits very difficult, so that officers there may have had to rely on control objectives to achieve greater surveillance of their clients. This pattern of objective specification made it tempting to define these agencies in terms of differential emphases on control- or health-related problems. Certainly, differences do exist in these objective areas.

Understanding the Use of Discretion in Risk Control

Initially, we believed that differences in supervision objectives for clients reflected differences in levels of client risk, and that consequently it should be possible to use risk levels as a basis for creating coherent groupings of offenders in terms of interventions. However, our analysis of objectives for three offender subgroups, shown in table 6-4, suggests minimal differentiation of supervision-objective type by risk. Although some slight patterns emerge—employment objectives are more pronounced in level-1 cases, health objectives in level-3—only employment objectives are related significantly to classification level.

Table 6-4
Percentage of Functional Objectives Specified for Probationers in Classification of Supervision Intensity: Big City and Eastern Suburbs

Functional Objectives	Level 3		Level 2		Level 1	
	Big City[a] (N = 153)	Eastern Suburbs[b] (N = 106)	Big City[a] (N = 304)	Eastern Suburbs[b] (N = 305)	Big City[a] (N = 171)	Eastern Suburbs[b] (N = 91)
Employment	22.9	23.6	31.9	22.0	35.1	27.5
Education	8.5	4.7	8.2	8.2	13.5	8.8
Social	21.6	23.6	18.1	25.6	18.1	24.2
Health	22.9	31.4	15.8	28.9	15.8	19.8
Control	24.2	17.0	26.0	15.4	17.5	19.8
Total	100.0	100.0	100.0	100.0	100.0	100.0
Percentage of cases	18.3	19.4	47.4	61.6	34.3	18.9

Note: The differences between the two organizations in the distribution of cases among risk levels probably reflect sampling bias. The Big City sample is a time-slice cohort; the Eastern Suburbs cases were hand selected by officers as typical cases, and it is likely that level-3 cases were underrepresented.

[a]$X^2 = 15.15$; $df = 8$; $p > .05$.
[b]$X^2 = 6.24$; $df = 8$; $p > .50$.

From our finding that risk level is generally not significantly related to supervision objectives (and, therefore, to tasks), we concluded that case-management systems that are based solely on risk will not substantially increase specialization in casework activity. In other words, the services, referrals, and nature of contacts for a caseload of level-3 offenders would not differ substantially from those for a caseload of level-2 clients. Thus, the higher risk of these clients does not necessarily result in different kinds of interventions necessary for risk control.

In discussing results such as these, it became increasingly clear that officers approached their supervision responsibilities from quite different points of view. Although it was possible to see why an officer specified a certain set of objectives in any individual case, we also wondered if predispositional cognitive "sets" led to differences in officers' supervision methods.

We were not wholly surprised by the existence of these differences. In her research on parole, Elliot Studt observed that parole officers have so much discretion in their day-to-day supervision of offenders that each officer becomes, for all intents and purposes, "the parole agency" to the client being supervised.[5] That is, as we pointed out in chapter 4, in determining their approach to supervision, community-supervision officers exercise extremely broad discretion about clients and daily tasks. By requiring our officers to specify behavioral supervision objectives, we made this aspect of probation supervision visible. The existence of this discretion led us to debate its implications for risk control in supervision. On the one hand, discretion is necessary to allow officers to identify appropriate risk-control interventions for supervising a client. Yet, to the degree it allows officers' attitudes and biases to determine interventions, discretion undermines the legitimacy of risk-control aims by allowing the arbitrariness of officer assignment to influence the way in which a case is eventually handled.

We decided to investigate the degree to which officers' patterns of objectives selection are a function of their attitude and background rather than of actual characteristics of the case. To control for differences that might have resulted from differences in the size or client characteristics of caseloads, we considered having a number of officers write objectives for the same set of clients and observing the resulting differences in case plans. This approach, however, would have been unwieldy for both officers and clients.

Instead, we decided to control for client effects by providing officers with an identical set of written case descriptions ("standard cases") and asking them to indicate which objectives they would specify for these clients. This method approximates normal supervision but does not re-create it. For example, officers would normally interview their clients before writing objectives for them. To overcome this factor as much as possible, we provided four to six pages of detailed information on each case. The effect of using only written data for specifying objectives is difficult to assess, although sentencing and parole research has used similar techniques with success.[6] One difference is apparent: probation officers tended to write more objectives for standard cases (about four) than for "live" cases (about three). This may have been because the level-1 classification occurred significantly less frequently in the standard cases than it does in actual probationer populations.

Because of the limited sample size (only forty officers) and nonrandom selection of officers, the results of this exploratory analysis resist generalization to all probation officers. However, the patterns of objectives selection that emerged suggested areas deserving additional detailed investigation, illustrated the problem of officer discretion, and provided insight into how objectives-based data can be used to help control that discretion.

The standard cases are summarized below from the simulated, lengthy presentence reports. Lower-than-average age levels were used for the standard cases because a significant proportion of the respondents were juvenile-probation officers.

Case 1: Henry Ward

Henry Ward is a seventeen-year-old white male convicted of second-degree assault. Ward has three prior arrests, including one for a felony (auto theft). His current offense involves an extended argument (lasting a week) with an acquaintance over a mutual girlfriend, culminating in a severe assault after a drinking episode. Ward has a history of transiency; his parents were divorced soon after his birth, and he was raised mostly by his grandparents. He received poor grades in school and was involved in numerous disciplinary incidents. His schooling ended with his expulsion and he expresses no interest in returning to school. He has been intermittently employed, is currently unemployed, and has no job skills. Psychological evaluation reveals high-average intelligence, indicates that his mother's influence is a "cause" of his delinquency, and concludes that he is "asocial and antiauthority." Ward is Catholic and has expressed an interest in further religious involvement. Except for bad teeth and a possible drinking problem, his health is good. He currently lives with his mother. Ward's previous probation was violated as a result of his school expulsion.

Case 2: Thomas Hill

Thomas Hill is an eighteen-year-old black male convicted of forgery. He has five prior arrests, one of which resulted in commitment to a juvenile institution (for burglary). The current offense involves forging a name to endorse a stolen payroll check. He was raised in a broken home but now has a stepfather. His living situation is one of poverty. He quit school in the eighth grade and is now employed full-time, earning sixty dollars a week. Hill has a low-normal IQ and is described as a "frequent cultural offender." Alcohol use appears to be his only health problem, although veneral disease may also be present. He has expressed an interest in obtaining a trade skill. Previous probation performance was satisfactory.

Case 3: Joseph Highfellow

Joseph Highfellow is an eighteen-year-old Native American male convicted of statutory rape. He has two prior "disorderly" convictions. The current offense involves the rape of his thirteen-year-old niece. He lives on a reservation, and little information about his home life or personal history is available. He attended the reservation school until the seventh grade and expresses no desire to go back. Highfellow is unemployed and works only during the summer as a farm laborer. He has a low-normal intelligence and is described as having "no social or personal ambition." The rape is seen as stemming from a reduction of inhibitions while intoxicated. He uses alcohol heavily, claims to lack relationships with women, and expresses little desire to improve his situation, although he reluctantly states he might consider attending school.

Case 4: Clark Fisher

Clark Fisher is a seventeen-year-old white male convicted of grand larceny. He has two prior arrests and one prior conviction for attempted robbery. His current offense involves breaking into a truck with some friends to steal cigarette-machine money. Fisher is the illegitimate child of a poor family— father unknown. His mother has a common-law relationship with a man who drinks heavily and whom Fisher intensely dislikes. Fisher's siblings have also been in trouble with the law. His life is described as "traumatic, deprived, unsocialized," and his criminality as "well rooted." He expresses an interest in completing school and is currently unemployed. He has no known emotional problems. He has avoided taking financial and personal responsibility for fathering two illegitimate children with a long-term girlfriend. He expresses little interest in religion. His health is good, except for a history of intermittent drug use. Prior probation performance was "very good." He currently lives with parents but wants to move out of the home.

Case 5: Richard Craig

Richard Craig is a seventeen-year-old black male convicted of robbery. He has three prior convictions for misdemeanors. His current offense involves taking money from a customer of homosexual prostitutes with whom he resides. He is an illegitimate child who was raised by foster parents, but left home because he did not get along with his foster siblings. He quit school in the ninth grade. Craig is unemployed but says he can get a job easily. He has a "deficient" intelligence and expresses no understanding of the basis for his criminal behavior. He wants to begin attending the Catholic church. Craig is in good health. He lives away from home and has a "shaky" relationship with a girlfriend who is pregnant with his child.

Supervision Discretion and Disparity

The standard-case information was created in order to approximate actual cases while presenting an array of differential data from which probation officers might select objectives. Table 6-5, which shows the distribution of the objectives written for the standard cases, reveals variety in the character objectives selected, as well as significant clustering. In fact, the degree of clustering is probably understated by the form in which the data are developed and the level of detail presented. Thus the difference between "get a new job" and "improve employment situation" might be important in terms of designing the tactics one might use in successfully securing employment in one case or changing the circumstance of an offender's present employment in the other, but on another level one might easily justify treating them as a single category. Further, it soon became clear in discussing results with officers that certain objectives were selected as the means to achieve other objectives. Thus, "enter or stay in a drug or alcohol program" often was selected as a method to "modify drinking habits." The means/end issue that this practice revealed became one of the important focal points of subsequent training efforts.

If just the combinations described were made, almost two-thirds of the objectives written would be located in no more than six categories in each case. But having said that, one must note that an important percentage of the objectives were distributed broadly and raised questions about their capricious nature. These cases that fell outside the clusters became a matter of particular interest to officers and the researchers. For example, in case 4, only one officer out of the forty raters thought it important that the offender "learn to read or write English." The officer choosing this objective was asked by his colleagues his reasons for choosing that particular objective. That inquiry set the stage for an important learning experience for that officer and resulted in a modification of his perception. In fact, the use of the standard cases were quite valuable as training vehicles and were used extensively in efforts to help officers learn about their own preferences and biases in the selection of objectives. They also provided a powerful tool to supervisors in approaching a discussion of the techniques of individual officers.

Table 6-5
Distribution of Descriptive Objectives Specified for Standard Cases,
by Forty Raters

Descriptive Objective	Standard Case				
	1	2	3	4	5
Maintain current employment	0	13	0	6	0
Get a new job	18	3	15	15	23
Improve employment situation	17	17	12	11	15
Return to or finish school	15	20	7	11	5
Get high-school-equivalency diploma	2	3	1	6	1
Reduce or curtail drug usage	1	2	0	14	0
Modify drinking habits	17	16	27	1	1
Enter or stay in drug or alcohol program	5	8	14	17	0
Improve relationship with certain person(s)	11	5	2	3	3
Terminate relationship with certain person(s)	9	6	2	6	10
Make new friends	5	2	1	7	3
Learn to read or write English	0	0	0	1	0
Report regularly and on time	2	8	7	6	6
Talk honestly and openly with probation officer	6	5	5	5	4
Accept referral to another agency	0	1	0	2	1
Get psychotherapeutic counseling	5	1	10	4	19
Attend group-counseling sessions	11	3	6	5	8
Get family counseling	8	0	1	5	4
Assume a specific financial responsibility	4	1	3	10	5
Deal with emotional problems	0	0	0	1	1
Get a new place to live	2	2	3	11	5
Accept residential placement	1	0	0	1	0
Live at home with parents or guardian	0	5	0	0	16
Become more assertive: improve self-image/self-confidence	0	0	3	1	0
Control anger/temper	5	0	0	0	0
Set goals/make life decisions	2	2	4	4	5
Use free time constructively	4	4	4	2	4
Improve financial situation	0	1	3	1	1
Curtail illegal activities	2	0	1	1	1
Accept authority of court; parent; probation officer	2	1	0	1	0
Get medical assistance: take medication	14	24	0	1	0
Attend church	3	7	1	1	3
Get driver's license	4	0	0	0	0
Cooperate with volunteer	3	0	0	5	0

There is not enough information on the effectiveness of supervision techniques to allow a determination of the optimal set of objectives that might exist in a given case.[7] However, when the number of objectives began to rise above four or five, officers felt compelled to justify that level of activity and set some bounds on the scope of their discretion. The visibility provided by the standard cases helped deal with the issue of supervision disparity—the establishment of indefensible supervision requirements primarily as a result of perceptual biases of an officer rather than as a response to real problems related to risks. Objectives did not create the problem—others have commented on its existence before.[8] However, objective-setting made the disparity visible and helped to illustrate its extent.

These results shown in table 6-5 left us and the officers interested in exploring whether officer background, philosophy, and work attitudes influenced objectives-specification decisions. To investigate this problem, we developed a set of measures of each of these three areas.

Correlates of Supervision Disparity and Discretion

Background Characteristics

Data were collected on the demographic characteristics of the forty officers: age, ethnicity (only one officer was black, and only one other had a Spanish surname), sex, years of experience in supervision, amount of education, and whether the officer had managerial responsibilities.

Attitude toward Correctional Policy

We used a variant of the *Correctional Policy Inventory*, the *Juvenile Justice Policy Inventory*. This questionnaire measures respondents' attitudes toward juvenile justice in relation to the two concepts of concern for offender and concern for community.[9] Dichotomizing these into "high" and "low" concerns yields four ideal-typical models of juvenile-justice policy.

In completing the questionnaire, each officer rated the statements associated with the four models for ten different correctional situations. The sum of the relative weightings for the items produced a total score for each officer for each model. This score indicated how closely the respondents' attitudes toward juvenile justice resembled a stereotypical policy model. The four policies are described briefly below.

The Reform Model. With a high emphasis on the community and a low emphasis on the offender, the reform policy stresses preventing the offender from being an inconvenience, risk, or financial burden to the community. Officers who score high in this model believe that the offender should exhibit behavior that conforms to accepted community standards, that stigmatization is justifiable to generate acceptable behavior patterns, and that staff should attempt to be "firm, but fair." They place little value on professional education; rather, the tendency is to hire "upstanding citizens" to supervise clients. Typically, reform-oriented staff use a great deal of discretion in decision making and respond to risk in an incapacitative manner.

The Rehabilitative Model. With a high emphasis on the client and less on the community, the rehabilitation policy focuses on improving the client's emotional functioning. Officers who support this policy tend to be concerned with responding to the cause of crime to identify the cause in terms of sickness in the offender. Their ideal staff are trained, skilled therapists who exercise a great amount of professional discretion in the supervision of client's progress toward self-understanding and self-acceptance. Most of the terminology—such as *diagnosis, prognosis,* and *treatment*—comes from the health professions and is used extensively in risk control.

The Restraint Model. With a low emphasis on both the offender and the community, the restraint policy attempts to make the offender-supervision process as smooth as possible. Officers who show a preference for this model believe that correctional supervision has little potential for changing the client's behavior; instead they focus on strengthening the correctional organization in order to maintain maximum independence from community interference. Under this model, staff tend to use organizational regulations as tools for minimizing potential conflict between the community and the agency rather than for risk control. Staff are expected to attend exclusively to their own work and to limit case activity to direct control-related supervision.

The Reintegration Model. With maximum concern for the offender and the community, the reintegration policy centers on the view that the offender who has a stake in the community is less likely to offend again. For staff who support this approach, developing that stake is the major goal of correctional supervision, and it may require changes in both the client and the community. This approach involves recruitment of a variety of staff. The focus is on developing supervision objectives that make sense to the client, since the client's genuine commitment to the supervision process is seen as essential for success. Emphasis is on long-term risk-control aims of treatment rather than on short-term incapacitation.

Attitude toward Casework

The final attitude measure rates officers on their attitudes about the roles of authority and assistance in the supervision process. *Authority* is defined as concern for exerting control over the offender during supervision. *Assistance* is defined as active concern for providing clients with direct services to meet their needs. Devised especially for this research, the authority/assistance questionnaire is based on a scale used by Glaser in his research on parole.[10] Its results were used to create two essentially orthogonal, six-level Guttman scales, one for the assistance dimension and one for the authority dimension.[11]

The variables assess the officers' background, attitudes toward correctional policy and attitudes toward casework. Table 6-6 lists the correlation between these characteristics and case objectives.[12] Although the small number of respondents involved makes it impossible to control further for some of the variables in order to develop an explanatory model, at an exploratory level. The correlations presented in the table indicate relationships between officer characteristics and objectives-selection consistent with impressions we gained through interaction with the officers. Officer-background variables appear to be related to patterns of objective selection. Younger, less experienced, and female officers, including those in non-supervisory positions, tended to write a larger number of objectives for the standard cases. Reintegrative-attitude scores are positively related to all objectives (both collectively and individually, except employment), whereas reform and restraint scores are consistently negatively associated with the objectives. Casework concern for authority is not related to objectives-selection patterns, but concern for assistance is consistently positively related to both type and number of objectives written.[13]

The results, then, indicate that the officer's background and attitudes influence the kinds of objectives he or she tends to select in supervising a case. This is not surprising; risk control is an ambiguous activity at best, and professional judgments are influenced by experiences and beliefs. Given the limitations inherent in the small sample size, two interesting characteristic patterns emerge from the data. First, several kinds of objectives appear to be strongly influenced by the amount of job experience a probation officer has. In fact officer experience and age may be significant influences in objectives-setting. Second, the measures used yield some evidence that there are two generalized groupings of officers. One group is characterized by a preference for a reintegrative approach, with an emphasis on assistance in casework, to the exclusion of reform/restraint philosophies. This group is better educated than the other and tends to write more objectives of almost any type. The second group shows a marked preference for reform/restraint philosophies (while re-

Table 6-6
Correlation Matrix of Officer-Background and -Attitude Variables and Objectives for Standard Cases

	Objectives						Casework Scale		Correctional Policy				Background				
	Employment	Education	Social	Health	Control	Total	Authority	Assistance	Reintegration	Rehabilitation	Reform	Restraint	Age	Sex	Experience	Supervision Responsibility	Education
Casework scale																	
Authority	-.04	-.11	-.12	.02	.08	-.06	1.0										
Assistance	.02	.28[a]	.17	.29[a]	.19	.32[a]	.21	1.0									
Correctional Policy																	
Reintegration	-.06	.23	.03	.33	.41[a]	.33	-.32[a]	.27	1.0								
Rehabilitation	.07	-.07	.18	.27	-.01	.20	-.25	.28	.25	1.0							
Reform	-.24	-.04	.16	-.23	-.53[a]	-.22	.40[a]	-.30	-.60	-.11	1.0						
Restraint	-.16	-.05	-.11	-.03	-.38[a]	0.23	.27	-.22	-.65[a]	-.19	.57[a]	1.0					
Background																	
Age[a]	.11	-.20	-.22	-.12	-.10	-.38[a]	.05	.29	-.14	-.46[a]	.22	.08	1.0				
Sex[b]	.26[a]	.16	.07	.24	.22	.42[a]	.30[a]	.16	.30	.14	-.20	-.06	.02	.10			
Experience	.12	-.31	-.36[a]	-.37[a]	-.10	-.34[a]	.27	.11	.26	.36	.23	.18	.76[a]	-.06	1.0		
Supervisor[c]	-.19	.32	-.01	.21	-.07	-.32[a]	-.08	-.31[a]	.07	-.49[a]	.04	.13	-.77[a]	.09	-.73[a]	1.0	
Education[d]	.05	.22	.06	.25*	.03	.19	.08	.29	.44[a]	.52[a]	-.04	-.39[a]	.31	.13	.14	-.13	1.0

[a] $p < .05$.
[b] = coded as male = 0; female = 1; Kendall's tau statistic.
[c] = coded as no = 0; yes = 1; Kendall's tau statistic.
[d] = Kendall's tau statistic.

jecting reintegration) and emphasizes the use of authority in casework. This group is less well educated.

For those who wish to control the use of officer discretion, this finding is potentially disconcerting. The thrust of professionalism, including inservice training and professional education, strongly supports the first group's approach. Like so many liberal criminal-justice reforms, however, this push for education, professionalism, and humanistic values may have the effect of increasing social control over the lives of offenders, even though this group's position may be preferable in several other ways to that of the second group. What is needed is a means of placing systematic controls on potential abuses of the professional model that may result from the tendency to intervene more frequently in clients' lives in a variety of ways.

It must be remembered, of course, that the selection of a set of objectives is very different from the act of supervising an offender using those objectives. Although there is clearly a relationship between both aspects of supervision, writing a set of objectives for a client should not be confused with the full meaning of engaging in the service/surveillance process of risk control. Nevertheless, the results of our analysis show a need for a routine approach for controlling the line officer. We began to explore how objectives setting could form the basis for that approach, based on an expansion of the unit supervisor's role.

The Strategy for Controlling Supervision Discretion

In light of the wide variation in officer approaches, we came to feel that it is the primary responsibility of the line supervisor to control officer discretion. This function requires positive involvement in the supervision process. Given the significance and inevitability of officers' use of discretion, the case-review function of the supervisor becomes crucial to the successful implementation of risk-control supervision.

The Supervisor as Manager: Case Review

Case review by line supervisors activates a frequently profound role conflict: the supervisor's identification with the line orientation versus the organizational goals. This conflict arises from the fact that almost all line supervisors begin their careers as line workers. Their frame of reference thus includes the predominant concerns described in chapter 4: control, case management, and competence.

A promotion to line supervisor requires an adjustment in role identification from line to management values. Many line supervisors have trouble making this adjustment, partly because they normally receive minimal guidance in the appropriate behaviors of their new role. Yet a change in view is critical, because no other person in the organization can successfully routinely review casework. To be effective as an organizational tool, review must center on concerns that reflect *organizational* aims as well as individual officer goals.

In terms of risk control, the organization's aims are quite explicit: identifying and supervising high-risk clients are the highest priorities. The officer is responsible for developing a risk-control supervision plan in the form of interventions designed to minimize the risk posed by the offender. Both incapacitative and treatment interventions become operational through the articulation of behavioral objectives. These objectives should address problems related to the client's risk (as opposed to officer biases), be reasonably designed to control the risk, and not be overly intrusive. The supervisor reviews the case plans of line staff to ensure that their actions adequately pursue these risk-control aims. As we have seen, there is evidence that an honest review of staff actions on cases will disclose staff biases and unique approaches that may not be legitimate without supervisory reinforcement of organizational goals, the goals are unlikely to remain a clear, central focus of officers' day-to-day work on cases; they will be replaced by the many and varying goal orientations held by individual staff. From the supervisor's practices, line officers learn that their decisions will be either unreviewed or closely scrutinized, case by case, to determine justifications in light of the organization's aims. Thus, the supervisor's role performance is a critical element of organic change.

But most supervisors are ill equipped to take this review role. First, both their career path and the dynamics of the office incline them to identify with line functions; physical proximity and a longer history of interaction with line staff often serve to strengthen line identification. Second, supervisors tend to feel isolated from managerial concerns, because they typically have little influence over organizational policies. The result is a tendency to have a greater tolerance for the line orientation toward supervision than for the organization's needs. The line orientation generally includes a desire for autonomy in decision making, since autonomy helps the officer to resolve the conflicts he or she faces. But managerial controls over autonomy are necessary if there is to be a clear pursuit of the organizational aims of risk control.

In response to this conflict, supervisors often assume a paperpushing role: they collect and review forms from staff, cajole staff into completing progress reports that are late, and review violations reports for form and content. In our experience, supervisors were important, despite the fact that their roles were extremely poorly defined and often appeared to be extraneous to day-to-day officer functioning.

The written case record system we designed for a behavioral objectives approach provided a tangible basis for revising that role, because it altered the technology of case review. First, it established a prospective focus for case review instead of the typical retrospective focus. Because the plan contains objectives, the supervisor can consult with the officer about their suitability very early in the supervision process. This approach also helps the officer as a result of the supervisor's involvement during the planning stage, the supervisor comes to share accountability with the officer for the substantive plans and results of supervision.

Second, and even more important, the written case plan made it possible to base accountability on organizational aims. The presence of specific behavioral objectives promoted intelligent, direct evaluation: Are the objectives sufficient for the case? Do they represent an unfair intrusion? Can each objective be justified in terms of humaneness, knowledge, and cost—that is, is the case plan consistent with the managerial policies of the risk-control organization? Finally, are the means chosen to achieve the objectives reasonable and the least intrusive necessary?

Thus, the supervisor provides a second opinion on risk-control measures adopted for the case, reviewing officer plans to ensure that the supervision effort is consistent with organizational aims as well as values. Through the objectives-based case plan, the supervisor becomes more aware of staff decision making, shares accountability for decisions, and exerts greater managerial control over staff. Objectives come to be as much a supervisory technology for role performance as a line approach to supervision.

**The Supervisor's Role in Organizing
Unit Resources**

Our change effort aimed not only at implementing a risk-control-oriented process but also at increasing the *effectiveness* of supervision in controlling risk. In addition to their role in maintaining officer focus on risk, supervisors have an even greater responsibility to increase supervision effectiveness, because they manage the most important level of community-supervision agencies—the level at which organizational resources are applied to clients. To increase the effectiveness of risk control, we had to revise the traditional organizational scheme, the generalist caseload. We also recognized the critical role played by the unit supervisor in this area.

In most community-supervision organizations, the assignment of cases is handled at the unit level and is administered by the line supervisor. Frequently, this task is routine—cases are assigned on the basis of geography, officers' caseload size, or staff-workload requirements. Supervisors assign cases on the basis of the information available to them. If information for case review is limited to activities—such as contacts and referrals—then activity requirements will predominate in the resource-allocation function. If additional information is available from the case plan—such as supervision objectives and risk level—resource allocation can effect a better fit between organizational aims and the specific problems of the client.

To address this area of unit functioning, we assessed current knowledge on the effectiveness of various resource-allocation methods. Our review provided a basis for understanding the importance of outcome information in organizing resources, since as Carter and Willkins put it

> The "numbers game"—be the number 15, 24, 30, 45, 50, 70, 90, or 100—is not significant in contrast to the nature of the supervision experience, the classification of offenders, officers, and types of treatment, and the social systems of the correctional agency.[14]

They advocate a "vertical model" of caseload organization, one

> based upon the view that not all offenders need equal amounts or intensities of supervision and the need for varying intensities or types of supervision. The high-success potential or low-need offenders are grouped into larger caseloads. The low success potential or high-need offenders are grouped into smaller caseloads. The high-low need and high-low success potential elements are estimated by the multi-factor classification.[15]

The result would be a series of different-sized caseloads composed of relatively homogeneous offenders. Grouping would occur on the basis of multiple factors indicating the level of supervision needed. A multifactor classification can be designed empirically, or it can be created expressly to include offense-related variables that reflect the desert requirements of a case.

A number of approaches have been developed to overcome the limited usefulness of caseload-size measures. One model that attempted a multifactor analysis is the "Work Unit Parole Program" of the California Department of Corrections, started in 1965. One of the goals of the program was to distribute the workload of parole officers more equitably so as to give "increased time and attention devoted to violent offenders and increased time for agents to accomplish the required tasks."[16] Parolees were classified into three groups: special (requiring more-than-average parole-agent time), regular (requiring moderate time), and conditional (requiring minimal time). Each case was then translated into work units, the estimated number of hours per month required for the case (4.8 units for special cases, 3 units for regular, and 1 for conditional), and each officer was assigned a workload not to exceed 120 units. Compared with regular caseloads, work-unit loads showed progressively lower prison-return rates into the mid-1970s.

Work units also appeared to be cost effective.[17] A recent adaptation of the work-unit concept for Wisconsin probationers and parolees had similar results.[18] The success of the work-unit concept stems from its attempt to direct staff activities toward cases on the basis of the client's needs for supervision. Other systems have been developed to identify the interventions staff should take with specific clients to improve supervision of cases.

The Environmental Deprivation Scale/Maladaptive Behavior Record (*EDS/MBR*), developed by the Probation Services Council of Illinois, has become a popular instrument for specializing supervision caseloads.[19] The *EDS/MBR* uses a behavioral analysis of several key areas of client behavior (such as school, employment, family, and friendships) to determine supervision-level needs. The analysis assigns points in each area, and the total score helps to determine the supervision level necessary for the case. Again, three levels of supervision are created, and assignments are made on a base-expectancy basis. The supervision level is then used to determine caseload organization and the distribution of cases to caseloads. For example, if a person receives supervision points because of problems identified in the employment area, the supervision task then becomes to remove these points and reduce supervision intensity through changing the status of the employment behavior problems.

Another system recently developed for probation and parole, the *Client Management Classification (CMC)*, uses a structured-interview format for assessing the client.[20] On the basis of responses in the forty-five-minute-to-one-hour interview, the client is placed in one of four major client groupings. Each grouping reflects a general client type and requisite supervision approach, and guidelines are provided for effective supervision of each client type. The "selective intervention" client, for example, is one who has committed an offense as a result of some single problem or life situation, and treatment of that problem alone is the primary suggested strategy. Thus, the *CMC* model classifies four general intervention strategies and uses a structured format to indicate which individual clients are best handled under each general strategy.

The work-unit-caseload models, *EDS/MBR*, and *CMC* all demonstrate greater attention to the *actions* taken with clients than to the number of clients in a caseload. This trend reflects a recognition that not all clients require the same amount or type of supervision. But this recognition of client diversity is not fully responsive to Carter and Wilkins's call for vertical caseloads that would represent homogeneous construction of cases. A decision to structure officer work with the cases on their caseload, however it is done, is not the same as a decision to structure the kind of cases placed on the caseload—that is, to provide for specialization.

The argument for specialization is a simple one: reducing the heterogeneity of activities an officer must undertake to supervise a caseload is bound to improve the overall quality of the more limited range of services provided by that officer. Having one expert on, say, finding employment will concentrate employment-related knowledge and resources in a way that serves clients better. No matter how well an assessment system may structure an officer's activities with each client, specialization in resource allocation will be an improvement over requiring every officer to play the role of jobfinder in some cases while also serving as counselor, referral agent, and the like in other cases.

The problem is that by focusing on *tasks*, supervision does not always sufficiently take into account the severity of the offense and the risk posed by the offender. On the other hand, focusing on *risk* often obscures the need to specialize officer functions within risk categories. Finally, the variety of work required in any ordinary caseload may negate the benefits of structuring work with each case. A recent national evaluation of intensive-probation projects recognized this problem in its recommendation that "the concept of caseload as a standard measure of degree of service provided probation clients should be replaced by measures of the quality and quantity of case contact."[21]

Although some of the systems summarized above can indeed improve the quality and quantity of officer-client contact, we believe that there are more effective alternatives to the general-caseload approach, however tasks are counted or structured. Measures of contact quality and quantity, for example, do not require specifically assigned caseloads at all; instead, functional areas (such as job consultant, welfare assistant, and family counselor) could be created for supervising clients with needs in these areas. The "Community Resource Management Team" (CRMT) has been developed as one alternative to caseload organization.[22] Its two key assumptions are that "established social work and psychiatric treatment" are ineffective and that "no one person can possess all the skills to deal with the variety of complicated human problems presented by probationers."[23]

Instead of staff generalists, the CRMT model creates specialists in skill areas—employment, counseling, legal assistance, drug abuse—but the emphasis is on direct purchase of services and provision of services through referral. Consequently, instead of cases, CRMT staff carry duty areas—functional responsibilities—for which they have expertise and are available to whatever clients need that expertise.

Despite the promising potential of this functional model, caseloads will continue to be popular modes of organization for supervisors. This popularity stems in part from the administrative convenience of caseload models—lines of authority are well established and clear for staff and supervisors, and case assignment is simpler. Responsibilities for paperwork, field activity, and rule enforcement are easier to determine in the event of a problem.

Using Objectives to Organize Resources

The popularity of caseload models also stems from the dearth of information available for making resource-allocation decisions. Models for case assignment such as CRMT do not take into account inevitable variations in officer approaches, nor do they address the very important differences in outcome goals for cases. This outcome information enables the supervision unit to specialize activities by focusing officer attention on a limited number and variety of objectives and by fitting the case-assignment decision to the special preferences and abilities of the officer.

The Big City project illustrates quite well how this efficient specialization can occur. During the fifteen months spent in organizational-design activities, staff met regularly to receive feedback about objectives and to discuss organizational philosophy in preparation for a reorganization effort. Despite the eventual emergence of an emphasis on risk-control concerns, it was also clear that different officers brought a wide variety of skills and interests to the supervision unit. One officer, regarded as especially skilled in intensive counseling activities, had in fact stopped seeing some of her caseload so that she could see a minority of cases more intensively. Other areas of officer interest and knowledge included drugs, the military, and language problems. One officer had developed a system of mail reporting for a large, noncontact caseload. The problem facing the supervisor was to make the best use of these existing officer skills and interests in the supervision of clients.

During the development of case-objectives data, it became clear from the number of objectives contained in the tables that specifying objectives did not automatically guarantee effective organization. Rather, the unit and researchers had to work together, pooling their knowledge and experience to interpret the data in ways that suggested new organizational models. This ambiguity was fed by the resistance to change that exists in any organization. After a reportedly fiery meeting (which the researchers did not attend), a subgroup designed an organizational model and the full group subsequently reworked it. Figure 6-1 shows the final format of this organizational model; we described some of its salient elements in chapter 5. In brief, the model called for a two-person intake effort involving initial case analysis, classification, and preliminary formulation of objectives. Supervision then flowed from assigned classification levels: one of the intake officers would handle level-1 cases on a low-reporting basis; a team would supervise level-2 cases; and one officer carrying a small caseload would handle level-3 cases on a counseling basis.

This model used information derived from the behavioral-objectives system, primarily data on cases classified as level 3. When early results in-

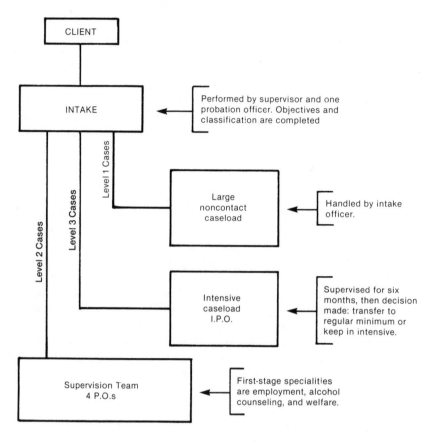

Figure 6-1. Proposed Big City Reorganization Model

dicated that these cases tended to show either good progress or no progress at all after six months of supervision, the unit decided to create a level-3 caseload that would handle these cases for only the first six months of supervision, after which they would be transferred either to the level-2 caseload (if there was some progress toward objectives) or to the level-1 noncontact caseload (for cases showing no progress at all). The large level-1 caseload would be administered by the probation officer who had helped the supervisor initially classify cases. A supervision team would supervise the level-2 cases on the basis of identified key objectives areas: one officer would develop jobs in the community for clients; another who had received special training in alcohol-related problems would carry primary responsibility for clients with alcohol difficulties; a third would serve as a liaison with welfare and medical agencies; and the fourth would carry an individual-counseling/group-counseling caseload. The entire supervision unit planned to meet weekly during the early stages of reorganization in order to make sure the organizational model worked smoothly.

The Big City experience demonstrates how data on cases can be used together with an understanding of personal skills and staff needs to redesign resource-use structures in community supervision. The staff approached the reorganization effort as an experience in problem solving, matching interests to client needs to create an optimal organizational model. The effort was organic in that the staff themselves, not an external person or group, designed the resulting change.

The result of these efforts has been a dramatic reconceptualization of the role of the line-supervision unit in community supervision. The supervisor is responsible for routine review of line-officer supervision plans so as to prevent abuses of discretion. It is also the supervisor's responsibility to organize the resources of line officers to increase effectiveness of supervision; this implies rejection of the traditional caseload.

The failure of caseloads may be due in part to the inadequacy of the assumptions that underlie their use, particularly the assumption that all probationers are essentially similar (a view often expressed in the same breath with advocacy of individualized treatment). Perhaps a greater failing was the general lack of fit between the traditional, randomly created caseload and the technology of community supervision. It is certainly a simple idea: different clients have different needs, and different supervision officers have different supervision skills. If this is so—and it is difficult to assume otherwise—then the traditional-caseload approach makes little sense. Moreover, in light of research indicating the negative effect of inappropriate treatment, the traditional caseload may even be counterproductive. Using his or her knowledge of both organizational goals and staff skills, the supervisor must take steps to reorganize for greater effectiveness.

To fit the organizational structure to the technology of supervision, some measure of technology that can inform organizational decision making is needed. Supervision objectives seem to meet this need. On the basis of our own research, we suggested several offender groupings. However, we have not elaborated a specific organizational model, because supervision objectives provide only one measure of the technology of probation. A full consideration of organizational alternatives must also take into account factors such as administration/management, court service, public relations, staff climate, and staff morale. Supervision objectives can, however, provide vital information for the formulation of a direct-service technology.

To describe a specific organizational design may be inappropriate for another reason: not all probation organizations attempt to meet the same technological needs. Differences in supervision technologies indicate a need for diversity in organizational styles for the varieties of probation agencies that exist. Moreover, flexibility accommodates changes in staffing and clientele. A supervisor making decentralized resource-organization decisions is best equipped to ensure diversity and flexibility. Thus, as the technology changes for an individual agency over time, the agency will, through the decisions of its supervisors, continually reassess its own organizational responses. As a systematic, standardized measure of the technology, behavioral supervision objectives can help routinize the continuing reassessment of the technology.[24]

This reconceptualization of the supervisor's role is twofold: first, the supervisor is the line-level control agent to ensure that supervision tasks are consistent with organizational aims. To augment this managerial responsibility, the supervisor must have responsibility for flexible use of unit resources through allocation of cases to staff. In each of these roles, risk-derived, objectives-based case plans are a primary support technology. In this new, larger role, the supervisor assumes many duties previously assigned to the administrator. This change is necessary for two reasons. First, the supervisor is more appropriately placed to carry out those duties. Second, as we shall see in the next chapter, the administrator must focus on a new set of responsibilities.

Notes

1. This understanding of technical change has been well described by Peter Vaill, "Reflections on Technology," *Social Change* 5 (1975):12-20.

2. In addition to court conditions, there was one other kind of non-supervision objective stated, representing less than 2 percent of the objectives. Called "life goals," these were supervision desires of the offender, worked on in the supervision process but not believed by the officer to be related to criminal behavior.

3. Leslie T. Wilkins, *Evaluation of Penal Measures* (New York: Random House, 1969), p. 25.

4. In making our categorization judgments, we used meetings with Big City probation officers to serve as a check on these judgments. For example, this group of officers first suggested the significance of the distinction between maintaining and obtaining employment. In a second, "blind" coding of objectives by graduate students, the student-researcher agreement rate for categorizing objectives was 95.1 percent for Big City cases and 90.9 percent for Eastern Suburbs cases.

5. Elliot Studt, *Surveillance and Service in Parole* (Los Angeles: University of California Press, 1972).

6. See, for example, Janet Katz, "Probation Officer Attitudes and Decision," *Criminal Justice and Behavior*, in press.

7. Arling and Lerner have developed a standardized classification system for identifying strategies that are useful for dealing with offender subgroups. Research is currently being conducted on the utility of this approach. See Gary Arling and Ken Lerner, *Client Management Classification* (Washington, D.C.: National Institute of Corrections, 1981).

8. See Citizen's Inquiry on Parole and Criminal Justice, *Summary: Report on New York Parole* (New York, 1974).

9. Vincent O'Leary, *Correctional Policy Inventory* (Hackensack, N.J.: National Council on Crime and Delinquency, 1967); idem, *Juvenile Justice Policy Inventory* (Hackensack, N.J.: National Council on Crime and Delinquency, 1969).

10. Daniel Glaser, *The Effectiveness of a Prison and Parole System* (Indianapolis: Bobbs-Merrill, 1964), pp. 429-41. The revision includes the ideology of reintegration in the measure of assistance, a concept that received prominence after Glaser published the original questionnaire.

11. A dichotomizing of these scales yields a correlation of .04 on pretest subjects. The correlation is slightly higher for probation officers who completed standard cases (.15), but still is not significant.

12. The latter represent nominal-level data, translated for ease of analysis into interval-level data by a count of the number of times a particular category of objectives appears in a case as well as the total number of objectives for all cases. This count can then be correlated with other, interval-level measures, such as the juvenile-justice-policy inventory score.

13. The influences of officer characteristics on cases varied among cases. Relationships between objectives and attributes produced by one standard case were often not reproduced even if the pattern remained strong when all the other cases were added together. Future research on the effects of differential officer backgrounds and attitudes on supervision behavior will have to take into consideration differences in clients being supervised. Because of our small sample size, we have reported only aggregate results.

14. Robert M. Carter and Leslie T. Wilkins, "Caseloads: Some Conceptual Models," in *Probation, Parole, and Community Corrections*, ed. Robert M. Carter and Leslie T. Wilkins, 2d ed. (New York: Wiley, 1976), p. 394.

15. Ibid., p. 399.

16. California Department of Corrections, "Work Unit Parole Program," mimeographed (Sacramento, 1973), pp. 4-5.

17. Ibid., p. 4.

18. S. Christopher Baird et al., "The Wisconsin Classification and Workload Project, *Report #2*, mimeographed (Bureau of Correctional Services, Madison, 1977).

19. W.O. Jenkins et al., *The Measurement and Prediction of Criminal Behavior and Recidivism: The Environmental Deprivation Scale (EDS) and the Maladaptive Behavior Record (MBR)* (Rehabilitation Research Foundation, University of California, 1972).

20. Arling and Lerner, *Client Management Classification*.

21. J. Banks et al., *Phase I Evaluation of Intensive Special Probation Projects* (Washington, D.C.: U.S. Department of Justice, 1981).

22. Frank Dell'Appa et al., "Community Resources Management Team: An Innovation in Restructuring Probation and Parole," mimeographed (WICHE Corrections Program, Boulder, Colo., n.d.).

23. Ibid., pp. 1, 2.

24. See David Duffee, *Correctional Policy and Prison Organization* (New York: Halsted Press, 1975).

7

Using Objectives-Based Community Supervision as an Administrative Tool

As an action-research proposition, we have stated the importance of viewing community-supervision organizations as sociotechnical systems. Recent work in the general area of management has supported this approach.[1] Traditionally, managerial literature has divided into two competing perspectives on improving organizational functioning: the scientific or technical strategy, which focuses on improving the effectiveness and efficiency of the technology of the organization,[2] and the human-relations strategy, which attempts to improve the quality of interpersonal interaction as a means of improving productivity.[3] Contemporary management writers point out that this strict dichotomy makes little sense, since both the technical and human aspects of any organization require attention for management to be effective.

This point relates directly to the problem of improving the administration of community supervision. In previous chapters, we have focused on technological approaches to supervision by addressing what Weisbord calls the "fit between the organization and the environment."[4] This congruence is achieved through establishing organizational "purposes and structure in order to support high performance and ability to change with conditions."[5] Thus, in part I we began with a critical review of the guiding purposes of community supervision. In part II, we identified an objectives-based technology for supervision consistent with those purposes and explored some methods for using that technology to make supervision more responsive to environmental conditions. The focus of much of this discussion has been the technology of community supervision (in particular the records system) using an objectives-based approach to case analysis and the evaluative functions of the agency.

Overemphasizing the importance of technology, however, may lead an organization to underestimate or ignore the importance of fit between individual and organization—"the extent to which people support . . . formal mechanisms intended to carry out an organization's purposes."[6] This is the human dimension of sociotechnical systems. Students of profit-making enterprise have observed the complex interdependence of technical and human factors in productivity. The widely cited General Electric studies indicate the limited importance of a solitary emphasis on technology for achieving productivity.[7] That there is a relationship between a person's feelings about his or her work and the quality of the work is undeniable. On

133

the other hand, "favorable attitudes and excellent morale do not necessarily assure high motivation, high performance, and an effective human organization."[8] Both dimensions are important; a failure both to provide for the human needs that operate within a work organization and to ensure that the technical structure of the organization is appropriate to its required tasks will result in limited effectiveness. If this is true for product-oriented business organizations, it is even more true for human-focused organizations such as community-supervision agencies, where so much of the operational technology is based on individual skills in human interaction. In the human-technology organization, to design a structural or procedural approach that interferes with the intrinsic motivators for high-quality work—no matter how rational or reasonable the structure/procedure may be—is to lay the groundwork for organizational conflict, stress, and, ultimately, failure.

The persistence of nonspecialized-caseload structures in community supervision despite well-documented evidence of their limitations illustrates the significance of human needs in service organizations. The apparently nonpurposeful distribution of cases in an office in fact does have a purpose: it distributes work in an essentially even manner and gives the surface impression that, since everyone is carrying about the same number of cases, each person is doing about the same amount of the organization's work.

For the manager, the simplicity of accountability under a caseload method is important; a clear basis exists for determining staff responsibility for updating records, maintaining the required number of contacts, and anticipating problems in cases. The bureaucratic utility of clear lines of authority should not be underestimated; indeed, the recently established American Correctional Association *Manual of Standards for Adult Probation and Parole Field Services* mandates them in several of its criteria for accreditation.[9]

Nor should the manager overlook the intrinsic rewards of a general-caseload approach for the line officer. If Frederick Herzberg is correct that job satisfaction in individual workers is closely related to the nature of the work itself,[10] then it follows that a change in job responsibilities for line officers will likely have implications for both job satisfaction and commitment to the work. The range of tasks required of the line officer who supervises a general caseload is quite broad. To some degree this very breadth may be an important factor in promoting job satisfaction. Specialization of functions and removal of casework authority might substantially reduce the caseworker's motivation to provide services.

The traditional casework approach has persisted, despite widespread and well-grounded criticism, in part because it is fairly simple to administer and, by giving line officers wide authority over a diverse group of clients, provides a sense of professionalism, responsibility, and control. Any change in the structure of community-supervision technology must not leave a substantial void in these areas, regardless of how rational it seems. One way to resolve this problem is to view the development of an objectives-specification technology as an organizational-change activity.

Managing the Objectives-Specification Process

Objectives-specification is basically what Chin and Benne refer to as an "empirical-rational" change strategy, one that is based on an assumption that "people are guided by reason and that they will utilize some rational calculus of self-interest in determining needed changes in behavior."[11] Objectives-setting is empirical-rational in several respects. The assumptions are largely cognitive: writing one's intentions helps to clarify them; summing up objectives provides a better picture of proper planning procedures; empirical evaluation of effectiveness is the best basis on which to make organizational policy decisions; and so on. The objectives-setting model is calculative, empirical, and based on logic.

But empirical-rational strategies have "worked better in developing and diffusing thing technologies than in developing and diffusing people technologies."[12] The danger is that objectives setting may become a mechanistic activity, with more impact on the surface operations of the probation agency than on the real activities of supervision and probation-department planning. Officers may give lip service to the objectives while supervising, planning, and evaluating clients on the basis of their day-to-day perceptions. In one organization we worked with recently, this proved to be the case: officers completed new forms for central administration, put them in the offender's file, and continued to supervise clients as they had in the past. No real changes occurred.[13]

The challenge, then, is to mold objectives specification into what Chin and Benne refer to as a "normative-reeducative" strategy, in which

> changes in patterns or practice are . . . not alone in the rational equipment of men, but at the personal level, in habits and values as well, and, at the sociocultural level, changes are alterations in normative structures and in institutionalized roles and relationships as well as cognitive and perceptual orientations.[14]

The goal is to get officers to feel ownership and control of the model as they use it. Two possible approaches to sharing objectives with the client illustrate the problem. On a rational level, sharing objectives can occur simply because it helps to achieve the objective. On the normative level, however, objectives-sharing occurs because the officer thinks it is both unfair and ineffective not to discuss and negotiate the supervision expectations with the client. The difference is one between normative changes, which have potential for long-term effect in supervision, and mere activity changes, which last only until other rationalistic approaches replace them.

In an effort to develop objectives-specification into a normative-reeducative change program, several human factors require consideration. Most important, an information system based on objectives must take into account the social aspects of the officer role. The variety of personal needs involved are at least equal in importance to the need for an orderly and consistent information system. For example, the officers need time to develop competence in writing objectives. Officers also need to feel their objectives should express their intent in supervision rather than their perception of the intent of researchers or administrators.

If long-term, high-impact changes are desired, the change process may be as important as the product. The change must be organic; officers must be involved in the "introduction, design, execution, feedback and evaluation of any and all aspects of the program."[15] This process requires time, but it helps ensure acceptance of and feelings of ownership for the final product. Through this developmental process, participating officers are more likely to accept the importance of objectives-specification and may become willing to experiment with the use of objectives and to engage in self-evaluation. Our work with community-supervision agencies produced these results consistently.

The best way of attaining the level of commitment necessary to effect objectives-setting as a normative change in agency technology is to involve the staff who will use it in every step of its development and implementation in the agency. This intensive involvement makes sense not only because the staff will best know the implications of the change for the specific supervision activity, but also because they will be responsible for making the system operational.

Objectives-specification methods are vulnerable to the passive resistance of capitulation without commitment precisely because they expose the *core* activity of the supervision process: the outcomes of supervision. Officers are bound to be sensitive to the uses made of this kind of data, despite efforts to be forthright about them. For example, in the Big City project, after a meeting one of the officers came to see us privately to express dismay; he hoped the data would not be given to the central office, lest they be used to fire or reassign officers. The feeling that administrative officers would misuse outcomes data was not unique to Big City. Line officers in most of our projects expressed misgivings about the visibility of the data to superiors. This unease was due to two factors. First, some of the officers had difficulty writing clear objectives and understandably did not want their inadequate work to reach the desks of superiors. More to the point, the data provided by objectives are imminently threatening to the people who produce them. When properly written, objectives eliminate window dressing from the goals of supervision by making desired outcomes explicit.

The patterns of some officers' objectives did indeed deserve attention from superiors; one Big City officer supplied more than half of the objectives requiring the client to "report regularly and on time" and more than half of those calling for the probationer to "speak honestly and openly to the probation officer." Her method of supervision—forcing clients to come in and "share feelings"—became visible and open to scrutiny by colleagues and superiors only as a result of objectives setting. This development did not harm the officer, who was widely perceived as having good skills in counseling; the staff decided instead to select appropriate counseling cases for her to handle. Moreover, when the officer realized that she tended to take this approach, she was better able to identify situations when it would be inappropriate for the client. Likewise, when another officer realized as a result of data-feedback meetings that he over selected drug-related objectives for clients, he was able to reduce reliance on these objectives. More difficult were situations in which the objectives-specification process exposed the fact that the officer simply did not know what he or she was doing with clients and could not begin to specify goals. These officers often wrote elaborate but meaningless objectives; some resisted writing any objectives at all and fell behind in case reporting.

There are several ways of knowing when staff are not using the objectives-based system maximally. Identically worded objectives will appear frequently in cases, with little attempt to fit them to the actual case situations; nonbehavioral objectives will be frequent and the variety of objectives smaller; fewer objectives will be stated for cases. The remedy is staff involvement at all stages of the innovation process. "Participation by subordinates in the planning process will increase their commitment to the goals . . . established."[16] Later, as the staff actually develop the instruments to be used, the change process itself can respond to staff misgivings, concerns, and questions. The process provides the occasion for staff to design into the change model their own "complex set of needs, *all* of which are important in . . . work and in life."[17] Each agency can adapt the objectives-based analytical model presented here to fit its own situation. Some may decide to change it substantially to suit their own internal and external environmental needs. This molding process, which gives credibility to the model, occurred in each of the projects reported in this study, and is continuing to occur in current projects. As long as staff are directly involved in this molding process, they will understand and accept the basis for the model and its potential applications.

To the degree that the case-diagnostic model is used as an aid to design organizational changes, it is also essential that staff be committed to the change.

Internal commitment means the course of action or choice has been internalized by each member so that he experiences a high degree of ownership and has a feeling of responsibility about the choice and its implications.[18]

Without internal commitment, the role relationships necessary to sustain change will not emerge. Again, to develop commitment requires participation, or, as Tannenbaum and Massarik have defined it, the ability actually to affect the outcome of decisions.[19] In Big City, the staff worked as a team to develop new organizational models based on objectives. This kind of involvement enabled them both to design into the new approach the same job satisfactions they had received from the caseload approach and to design *out* some sources of ineffectiveness and frustration. Although this effort took a long time, it increased the commitment to change. Involvement in all phases of development means that staff should help design the data-recording instrument and conduct the service-delivery surveys. The format for data feedback and the problem-solving process for organizational design should reflect staff input. The manager is involved in each of these decisions, but the results must reflect the needs of both managers and staff.

This intensity of cooperative effort assumes that an organization has developed "interpersonal competence."[20] Likert characterizes "healthy" organizations as those in which there are a sharing of power and authority in decision making, a high degree of staff communication, and the involvement of subordinates in organizational governance.[21] Because of the administration's potential for subverting meaningful change, autocratically or authoritarian-managed community-supervision agencies would do well to address the style of administration before attempting any major changes in technology. In an environment conductive to a high degree of participation, technological innovations have more potential for being effective.

Links to Other Management Technology

For healthy organizations, objectives-specification models provide a link to a variety of current management technologies. Four new approaches discussed below illustrate the salience of risk-control objectives-setting in promoting better management practices in community supervision.

Management-Information Systems and Accountability

At the core of a system's operations is the information it collects and stores. Information provides the basis by which a system can determine whether it should continue operating as it has or adjust to new environmental and output requirements. It is through information that a system is able to monitor its own actions. Consequently, effective management of a system depends on the quality of information available for decision making.

A system needs to know not only what its activities are (how it is "spending" its resources), but also the meaning, effect, and value of its activity selections. As C. West Churchman has put it, "one cannot use the amount of physical activity as a measure of performance of a system. One has to show how the activity is translated into a measure of utility or value."[22] Community-supervision agencies need measures of the performance—the value added—of the system. Lacking such a system, they often attempt to increase activity (smaller caseloads, more contacts, more officers) instead of selecting more effective activity.

David Duffee, in researching change strategies in prison systems, found that the failure of contemporary change efforts in areas such as higher education, inservice training, and laboratory training had significance for corrections.[23] In Duffee's view, these reforms have failed because they aimed at attitudinal dimensions of members of the organization rather than at changing the technology the organization uses. Duffee saw a need for new change strategies that would involve

> rebuilding the organization rather than adding pieces as new problems appear. Rebuilding should begin with the development of new models that have a more logical relationship to the kinds of goals correctional organizations are now trying to achieve. . . .[24]

The result will be organizations that are

> free to change internally in order to meet any specific problems that are brought to it. This kind of organization . . . responds to newly presented problems in terms of experience with applying processes of problem solution that have been effective in the past.[25]

Objectives-specification may play a role in developing that kind of organization. Many current information systems in community supervision attempt to keep data on client contacts, caseload movement, and the like—activity data. Objectives can serve as system-performance data, measuring the things of value (such as new offender behaviors) that are produced as a result of supervision. They also have potential as feedback on larger effectiveness issues. By relating specific behavioral changes to recidivism data, it may be possible to generate a learning system that develops information about which treatment goals, when accomplished, appear to be useful for reducing the criminality of different kinds of clients. For example, many clients have multiple problems. Systematic analysis of client performance will help to indicate what problems are most directly related to eventual law-abiding behavior.

The management-information system should also tie in with measures of accountability. Naomi Brill has commented that we live in

"the age of accountability." Accountability is demanded by critics both within and outside of systems, who are concerned by the increasing dimensions and severity of social problems, by the apparent ineffectiveness of old methods and programs, and by the demand for increased resources to implement these services.[26]

Within the system, accountability simply means the selection of appropriate and effective interventions. External accountability, however, is the basis on which the system is able to justify its expenditures of funds. That is, the system must be able to produce evidence of its productivity in order to show the need for continued funding. In these days of tight budgeting, accountability may be the lifeblood of the social-service agency.

To provide data on areas for improvement and to justify requests for increased funding, the agency must be able to identify not only key services delivered but also key services *not* delivered. The behavioral-objectives system, by identifying objectives not met, thereby provides data on resources that were not successful. By identifying ineffective resources, the community-supervision system can identify areas where change may be needed to improve supervision effectiveness. Accountability can also be made hierarchical: staff are accountable to supervisors for achieving objectives, supervisors are accountable to administrators, and administrators take production data to funding sources to justify continuation or increases of funding.

In this way, accountability is a product of the information system (through the collection of useful data), of outcome specification at the line level, and of measurement issues that require the articulation and measurement of reasonable goals.

Management by Objectives

Management by objectives (MBO) was first developed as an approach to administration by Peter Drucker in the 1950s.[27] Since then, the model has become extremely popular and has been applied to a variety of organizational settings. Because of these numerous applications, several versions of this approach exist.

Quite often, MBO is viewed as an objective-setting process, and no more. At other times it is interpreted as an approach to performance appraisal. Some practitioners regard MBO as essentially a management development program. Others have construed MBO to be a tool that is useful in determining executive compensation. Still others consider the concept to be synonymous with manpower planning. MBO is none of these, or, more appropriately, is all of this—and more. The common error is to define the concept too narrowly and consequently practice, in the name of MBO, only a part of it. Follow-up studies on firms that have reported unsuccessful experiences with MBO have revealed that they were not practicing MBO but one of the limited programs described above.[28]

MBO is a broad management approach that has impact on "the five basic management functions—planning, organizing, staffing, leading and controlling."[29] Odiorne has defined the basic component of MBO as a

> process whereby the superior and subordinate managers of an enterprise jointly identify common goals, define each individual's major area of responsibility in terms of results expected of him, and use these measures as guides for operating the unit and assessing the contribution of each of its members.[30]

Thus, MBO is a management system that parallels the supervision approach of objectives setting. Both are result oriented rather than activity based; both are useful as tools for planning and evaluation; both include in their function the clarification of organizational purposes. What officers do with clients in objectives-setting for supervision is a line-level example of the process and interactions of staff members in MBO. In fact, failure to specify case objectives might limit the potential of MBO as a correctional tool, despite increasing pressure to adopt it in the public sector.[31] One critic of nonprofit applications of MBO has expressed this concern:

> It is more difficult to set goals in the public service setting. Goal setting is easier if we can see if we have improved profits or increased sales or increased stock values. Measuring services, however, is not so simple: How do you measure the value of educational release programs, of a halfway house, of vocational training, or of scores of correctional programs.[32]

Of course, correctional programs are quite capable of setting organizational objectives that would oblige the agency "to increase the number of high school diplomas granted at the end of a selected instruction period,"[33] but how are decision makers to know whether such an organizational goal is appropriate? Organizations may set objectives that, even when needed, have little bearing on the formal mission with client.

Melvyn Raider has recognized this issue as one of two major problems in MBO applications to social-service agencies. In adapting the model directly from nonprofit organizations, many have maintained the deductive procedure common to industry, whereby "goals are established by the department head (and) somewhat specific goals are derived from the more general, global mission."[34] For a variety of reasons, this process needs to be reversed in the human-service agency.

> Goal development should be an inductive process in a social service agency. General departmental or unit goals are constructed from the many detailed individual worker objectives. After compiling individual worker objectives, members of the department would collectively seek to ascertain what common goals could be formulated and what plans could be developed.[35]

This is an ideal role for supervision objectives. If, for example, client objectives in an agency indicate that, taken collectively, education objectives are frequently rated as critical in importance but are seldom accomplished, the agency may wish to establish higher-level organizational objectives and devise some action plans to change this condition. Other organizations with different supervision problems, as indicated by the client objectives, would wish to write other organizational objectives. The organizational objective, then, becomes a statement of broad results necessary to assist officers in working with individual clients and their objectives.

Because the broad mission of the organization is important, this process is not solely inductive. Instead, this is a two-way feedback process. Information on cases flows upward. Organizational members determine agency objectives on the basis of both information and the general mission. These agency objectives, in turn, influence and help to guide case decision making. When done at all levels of the organization, objectives-setting can perform this integrative function.

One final point about MBO deserves mention. John Humble has pointed out that the failure to involve in its establishment those affected by an objective is the leading cause of the failure of MBO systems.[36] This factor underscores the need for staff participation in the objectives-setting process and also suggests the need to involve clients directly in that process.

Zero-Base Budgeting

Zero-base budgeting, a method developed by Peter A. Pyhrr, uses the organizational-budgeting process as a means of planning and controlling organizational processes and of promoting innovation and change.[37] It is called "zero-base" because it requires each part of the organization to justify its budget (the level of commitment of organizational resources) in terms of cost/benefits. Roughly speaking, each component of the organization begins the budget year with a budget of zero and must justify any additional financial support in terms of overall organizational gain. A brief outline of this elaborate process illustrates its links to case objectives-setting.

In the budgeting process, the organization is broken down into "decision packages" that identify "a discrete activity, function or operation in a definitive manner for management evaluation and comparison with other activities."[38] A decision package includes at least the following: the purpose of the activity, the consequences of not performing it, measures of performance of the activity, alternative courses of action, and the cost of the package. Managers then make a decision whether or not to "buy" the package (that is, include it in the budget). If they do not, they will at least understand the consequences of not funding the package.

Two aspects of decision packages are important for effective decision making. First, each package must state alternative approaches to achieving the purpose (usually contained in parallel decision packages). Second, the package must include a "levels-of-effort" statement, which places an activity at several alternative funding levels (for a greater or lesser degree of performance of the function) and describes the costs and benefits of each level of funding. Thus, the manager selects both from a variety of alternative ways of achieving a function and from a variety of levels of funding one means for achieving that function.

Determination of the final budget stems from ranking the various decision packages on the basis of priority of need for the function. A moderate-sized organization may have as many as thirty to fifty decision packages, ranked individually from most important to least important.

Although zero-base budgeting was originally developed for private industry, "the philosophy and procedures used to install zero-base budgeting in industry and government (as well as the benefits obtained and the general problems faced) are almost identical."[39] In community supervision, for example, decision packages could reflect levels of supervision (such as caseload sizes), addition of specialized personnel (job counselors, family therapists), provisions for contractual services (placements and referrals), and so on, in addition to administrative functions.

These decisions of personnel deployment are of both budgetary and policy significance. For example, the level of contacts necessary to establish the minimal level of effort for supervision—and the requisite size of caseloads—is open to question. Also open to debate are such issues as: how resources should best be arranged to determine service levels; the relative need for specialists in service areas versus contracting for services; the relative importance of a job training specialist; whether paraprofessionals would perform as effectively and at less cost many of the functions now done by line officers; and whether budget monies should be made available for other important functions.

The zero-base budgeting process makes it possible to address all these issues quite naturally. Supervision objectives can help to determine what goes into the packages and packages priorities. For example, an agency may want to purchase job-trainee positions for some offenders and psychiatric assistance for others. The zero-base approach requires arranging these at different levels of effort (in this case, the amount of money needed to buy a certain number of services). Collective supervision objectives help to determine what levels of funding are in fact minimal, what is full funding, and what ranking each alternative should have on the basis of client need. The result is a direct link between supervision objectives and the intent and rankings of decision packages.

Two factors are important in building a successful zero-based budgeting system. First, the agency's mission and policies related to that mission need to be clear to those who build decision packages. This is not to say that the policy should determine the packages.

> Members are sometimes constrained by general policies and procedures . . . over which they have no direct control. Instead they should be encouraged to develop their decision packages and rankings on merit alone, highlighting any recommended changes—such as in policy—to top management.[40]

Allowing this flexibility will help ensure the potential for organization growth.

The second point must by now sound like a litany: those who are affected by a budgeting decision must be allowed to develop the decision packages that reflect the areas within their managerial control. This means that the packages will reflect the knowledge about minimal levels and alternatives of those who have responsibility for implementing the functions. It also creates a widely shared responsibility for and knowledge of the organizational-budgeting process.

Program Planning

Two general approaches to program planning are useful in needs assessment: single-event needs analysis, which aims at discovering, at a specific time, the resource needs of a population of offenders; and routine (or ongoing) needs assessment, a more sophisticated method of determining both the effectiveness of programs and additional program needs for a given agency. Which method is appropriate depends on the characteristics of the agency using them and on the problem at hand. Single-event needs assessment can be conducted as a one-time project and requires no reorganization of record keeping; therefore, it may be more relevant to smaller agencies with limited funding and flexibility. Ongoing-needs assessment requires an investment of time in developmental processes, redesign of records, and data-processing capabilities; thus, it may be more appropriate for larger agencies committed to a program of organizational development. A benefit of the second approach is that it provides the agency with a basis for measuring environmental contingencies and shifts in client population, and therefore supports the organization's continuing adaptation to task requirements.

Single-Event Needs Assessment. In the summer of 1974, we conducted a single-event needs assessment in Eastern Suburbs. An umbrella agency for a consortium of five district courts had received substantial funding for new programs for the clients of the courts. The agency needed a rationale for funding specific programs. Some of the monies had already been spent for officer-requested contractual services (such as summer camp), and it was felt that a more organized expenditure of monies would increase the effect of the funding. A research team from the School of Criminal Justice, State University of New York at Albany, conducted a four-step needs-assessment project.

Step 1: Determination of Resources and Services Currently Being Requested and Used. The objectives-based format was used to select and analyze a nonrandom sample of 190 current cases. In addition to listing and rating the actual resources being used, officers were asked to *describe* the ideal resource needed for each objective. This process yielded an objectives-based listing of risk-control needs.

Step 2: Development of Resource-Needs Instrument. Based on the resources identified in step 1, an instrument was developed to specify the resource needs for a random sample of about 250 cases each of adults (a 33-percent sample) and juveniles (a 10-percent sample). The instrument, to be completed by the officers supervising these cases, called for a risk classification and a rating of the need for and quality of the resources available to meet the cases' risk-control needs.

Step 3: Client Interviews. While the supervision officers were completing the survey instruments as described in step 2, the agency conducted a series of interviews of step-1 clients. One objective of these interviews was the development of a listing of resources the offenders believed would help probation clients "stay out of further trouble with the law."

Step 4: Resource Planning. In a three-day planning session, a group of probation managers and representatives of line staff (those who had participated in step 1) analyzed the data derived from the steps above. The group identified general priority areas for funding and then divided into task forces for each of the priority areas. The task forces were to formulate specific programs or approaches for meeting client needs in each priority area.

Tables 7-1 and 7-2, which present the results of the Eastern Suburbs single-event resource survey, illustrates the kinds of data derived from such a project. Table 7-1 lists the ten resource areas identified for clients that were most frequently rated as poor in quality or not available. Table 7-2 lists the

Table 7-1
The Resource Categories Most Frequently Rated "Poor" or
"Not Available" for Adults and Juveniles

Resources Needed	Number of Cases[a]	Percentage Rating of Cases				Number Rated Rated Poor or Not Available[a]
		Good	Fair	Poor	Not Available	
For adults:						
Job counseling	300	.07	.13	.40	.40	240
Full-time job	250	.24	.04	.24	.48	180
Individual counseling	510	.27	.43	.22	.08	150
Job training	90	.11	.00	.33	.56	80
Drug counseling	150	.27	.33	.20	.20	60
Clinical screening/ diagnosis	90	.22	.11	.22	.45	60
High-school equivalency	100	.40	.00	.30	.30	60
Alcohol counseling	220	.23	.55	.18	.04	50
Single-person housing	80	.12	.25	.63	.00	50
Educational counseling	60	.17	.00	.33	.50	50
For juveniles:						
Individual counseling	243	.48	.30	.16	.06	54
Educational counseling	75	.12	.44	.28	.16	33
Group home	54	.33	.05	.50	.12	33
Part-time job	93	.45	.23	.23	.09	30
Employment	42	.08	.21	.50	.21	30
Family counseling	198	.53	.33	.08	.06	27
Special-curriculum school	75	.56	.08	.20	.16	27
Job training with pay	33	.18	.00	.45	.37	27
Sports and recreation	60	.45	.20	.20	.15	21
Counseling for parents	84	.57	.18	.07	.18	21

Source: Vincent O'Leary, Todd R. Clear, and James Fox, "Eastern Suburbs Probation Service Project Needs Assessment Survey: Summary Report" mimeographed (State University of New York, School of Criminal Justice, Albany, 1974).

[a]Estimated from sample.

ten resources mentioned most frequently by clients in the interviews.[41] On the basis of these data, the probation officers identified four areas of concern: employment, education, recreation, and housing.

> The officers also noted the heavy emphasis on counseling needs, but it was their feeling that a good deal of this was related to such other factors as employment and schooling adjustment and they did not call for significant resources to be expended on direct counseling assistance.[42]

Table 7-2

Ten Resource Categories Most Frequently Mentioned as Needed, by Ninety-One Probationers in Interviews

Resource	Frequency	Percentage of Cases
Local recreational facility	39	42.9
Job-placement programs	33	36.2
Job-training programs	23	25.2
Informal counseling (noncourt)	13	14.2
Outdoor recreational facilities	11	12.1
Alternative educational programs	10	10.9
Financial assistance	8	8.9
Alcohol treatment (non-AA type)	7	7.8
Outdoor recreational groups	6	6.7
Drug-counseling programs	6	6.7

Source: Vincent O'Leary, Todd R. Clear, and James Fox, "Eastern Suburbs Probation Service Project Needs Assessment Survey: Summary Report," mimeographed (State University of New York, School of Criminal Justice, Albany, 1974).

The need to improve employment-related resources was seen as most important; accordingly, a decision was made to "link up the five departments to existing and emerging manpower training and placement efforts and it was strongly suggested that some type of liaison group on manpower development be established among the five departments."[43] In the area of recreation, it was decided that short-term special projects "would not be nearly as far reaching or lasting as a united effort by the five departments to articulate the needs of young people . . . and to bring about heightened sensitivity to the need for change."[44] For housing and transportation, it was decided to create a "central fund which might be expended on an immediate voucher basis."[45]

What is important is not the results of the need survey; none of the participating officers found them particularly surprising, although they would probably have disputed the exact ordering of priorities had the data not been available. The data served to *underscore* need areas, and, perhaps more important, showed that some "pet" need areas (such as drugs/alcohol) were not nearly as central as many of the officers intuitively believed. In operating agencies, where breaking the existing equilibrium of day-to-day work is so difficult, these data provided the impetus for systematic resource development and, by providing empirical support for change, became a catalyst for organizing change efforts. Before the resource-planning meetings, the tendency had been to use funds to purchase recreational services and occasional places in job-training programs. The survey made it possible to develop some broad, community-wide strategies for resource improvement.

Our involvement in this single-event resource study led us to identify some elements crucial to conducting a successful survey. First, the resource-identification activity should be objectives-based. The strategy involves more than officers' creation of a list of resource areas. Rather, the listing of resources must be linked directly to expected risk-control outcomes of the supervision process. The composite field of resources is established by surveying the actual resources needed to achieve specific objectives for a sample of cases. This approach ensures that the resources surveyed will be result oriented and, more important, it helps provide a comprehensive array of community resources.

Second, it is essential to recognize the expertise of the supervision officers and allow it to influence the planning processes. In the early stages of the project, some of the officers expressed concern that their opinions would be of little importance in the ultimate policy decisions, that instead numbers would determine how money was eventually to be spent. These concerns were a source of some officer resistance to the research effort. In fact, to use empirical results without the informed interpretations of people from a variety of backgrounds and perspectives reduces the usefulness of the resource-development process. The manager who has need-survey data readily available for planning should not ignore related input from subordinates. These data should serve as a tool for stimulating, organizing, and increasing human input into decisions.

That does not mean that decision makers should undervalue the information provided by numbers. Individual officers, in the performance of their work, know all too well that resources for many clients are inadequate or nonexistent. But this information, obtained experientially on a day-to-day basis, is difficult to quantify and to subject to systematic inquiry. Officers' daily responses to these frustrations often come across as not much more than complaints. In this context, numbers wield an influence that is difficult to ignore. Proportionate estimates yielding projected numbers of cases suffering from insufficient resources become a clear and urgent signal to county commissioners, agency managers, and others who deal in community-resource development. Although empirical results alone do not guarantee change, statistics can frequently initiate the necessary steps for change.

The single-event approach does have several limitations. Most obvious is that client populations and environmental constraints will change over time, and new program-development priorities will emerge. To assess these, a new resource survey will be necessary. Thus, given the fact that replications are inevitable, the single-event approach might be more accurately described as an occasional-event resource-survey approach.

A second weakness is that the primary focus on resources is likely to overidentify resource needs; that is, officers will identify some resource areas that are in reality only marginally related to the risk-control requirements of a case. To the degree that this overidentification is frequent and systematic, it is likely to result in development of resources that are less than central to risk control. This effect is ultimately destructive of the organization's overall mission.

Nevertheless, the single-event approach has benefits for small or dispersed agencies. These agencies, particularly if they already use objectives-based recording methods, will find single-event approaches manageable, since they require no computerization (all computations can be done by hand) and can be completed by one or two persons over a short period of time. In addition, because the approach is particularly suited to identifying one or two target areas for activity, it may be most realistic for the smaller agency.

Routine Needs-Assessment Methods. The routine needs-assessment model integrates objectives-based case planning systems into the regular operations of the agency. Therefore, this approach is probably most suitable to the large agency using a variety of resources to serve a diverse client population. To get maximum benefit from a routine needs-assessment model, the agency must have its own computer-programming resources.

Daniel Glaser has provided an excellent discussion of the potential of agency-operations records for evaluative research.[46] The points he makes are valid for objectives-based recording systems, because program-evaluation purposes are directly linked to resource-planning and development decisions.

According to Glaser, evaluative research has not been well integrated into agency functions. Several reasons for this stem from the traditional antagonism of research and operations-information needs. Research and evaluation are too frequently seen as outside activities not related to direct-service activities. Thus, when staff fill out extra forms for externally motivated research, the data are often incomplete or inaccurate: "When those who fill it out are not likely to see the form again or be reprimanded if their entries are inaccurate, one cannot expect good data collection."[47]

The alternative is to use the agency's operations records as a source for evaluative data. These records are more likely to be accurate, since the officer is often evaluated by the quality of written work and therefore has a larger stake in the data. Unfortunately, agency records are bulky, inefficient to use, and are "not designed for research."[48] Often they take the form of sequential narrative summaries without a standard format, and consequently "it is extremely difficult for officials to test their validity."[49]

Glaser suggests that "the remedy for these problems with narrative reports . . . is to have precoded reports in standard categories which staff can simply check to indicate the information they wish to report."[50] This system might work for presentence-investigation reports, but precoded supervision reports might lose their vitality. For example, a checkoff objectives system is likely to result in an increase in the number of objectives listed. But the translation from raw objectives to descriptive categories is not difficult and could be done reliably by one or two agency staff. Moreover, objectives could be written in unique forms and later be related by the officer to generic areas of client functioning through a checkoff scheme. Either procedure would retain the necessary vitality of uniquely worded objectives while allowing coding of categories for purposes of evaluation and planning.

Once this information—objectives, importance, resources, and progress—is computerized, the potential for continued regular evaluation of agency output is excellent. For purposes of both administration and evaluation, only a small amount of additional information need be collected: disposition of case, arrest/jail date, demographic data, case processing dates, and so on.

Objectives-based data are more performance related than data now recorded and analyzed in many agencies ("input" data about the offender and offense and rough output data—usually type of termination). In the former case, the agency is keeping data on performance of offenders, behavior changes achieved, and resources used, making "collection of many of the data needed in evaluative research automatic as a part of operations requirements."[51]

Galbraith has pointed out the potential of regularly updated offender-progress evaluations for systematic research.[52] Changes in performance over time will provide information on optimal release times; interactions between types of offenders and treatment programs may also be studied. (For example, do younger offenders in particular programs do better than older ones?) Spurious programming might be exposed. (For example, do offenders who complete educational objectives during supervision have no better success rate than those who fail to achieve those objectives?) Systematic analysis of objectives-based data allows investigation of different approaches to supervision intervention.

For the community-supervision agency, evaluation serves primarily as a key step in the planning process. Evaluations are conducted to provide the information needed to establish changes and plan future approaches, including identification of resource-need areas.

The potential of objectives-based systems for improved planning is clear from our experience with progress ratings in the Eastern Suburbs and Big City samples. Officers in both agencies were asked to rate the progress made by clients toward achieving objectives. Big City officers rated progress on a quarterly basis as a part of their routine information system, starting with the second quarterly report. Eastern Suburbs officers rated progress on objectives ten months after the initial report. Table 7-3 shows the distribution of progress ratings for objectives receiving twelve or more ratings from Big City and Eastern Suburbs probation officers. No recurrent patterns of progress on objectives emerge between samples. Types of objectives with

Table 7-3

Progress Ratings on Objectives by Descriptive Categories Having Twelve or More Ratings: Big City and Eastern Suburbs

Descriptive Objective	Percent Achieved		Average Progress Score		Number of Objectives Rated	
	Big City	Eastern Suburbs	Big City	Eastern Suburbs	Big City	Eastern Suburbs
Get a new job	21.4	33.3	2.61	3.30	28	69
Improve employment/get job training	16.7	23.5	2.56	3.06	18	34
Return to or finish school	18.9	24.1	2.62	3.17	16	29
Reduce or curtail drug usage	50.0	19.0	3.00	3.38	12	26
Improve relationship with certain persons	25.0	18.9	3.17	3.08	12	37
Maintain current employment/ improve job performance	57.6	—	3.93[a]	—	33	—
Accept authority of parent; court; probation officer	—	21.1	—	3.68	—	19
Use free time more constructively	33.3	27.8	3.00	3.28	12	18
Modify drinking habits	—	17.6	—	3.38	—	29
Report regularly and on time	8.7	—	3.00	—	23	—
Talk honestly and openly with probation officer	5.3	—	2.89	—	19	—
Get psychotherapeutic counseling	—	33.3	—	3.50	—	18
Deal with emotional problems	—	11.8	—	3.35	—	17
Get a new and stable place to live	—	37.5	—	3.12	—	16
Enter or stay in drug or alcohol program	—	20.0	—	3.27	—	15
Become more assertive: improve self-image/self-confidence	—	14.3	—	3.14	—	1
Set life goals/make certain life decisions	.0	—	2.62	—	13	—
Total[b]	24.9	24.6	3.03	3.25	278	46

Note: — = fewer than twelve ratings given in sample.

Note: Progress was rated on the following scale: achieved = 5; good = 4; some = 3; little = 2; none = 1.

[a]Difference from total mean = $p < .01$ using F-test.

[b]Total of all objectives rated.

significantly different progress ratings in one sample show no significant differences in the others. However, some common patterns appear in the direction of the relationships. For example, "get job training" and "return to or finish school" show lower-than-average achievement. Likewise, "reduce or curtail drug usage" has a slightly better, though nonsignificant, progress rating. On the whole, however, systematic patterns are not apparent.

For example, "get a new job," which shows significantly less progress in the Big City sample, has a mean rating almost identical to the overall mean in the Eastern Suburbs sample. Again, in the Big City sample, two categories relating to employment show opposite, statistically significant, progress ratings ("get a new job" is linked to little progress, whereas "maintain current employment" is linked to achievement).

Table 7-4 summarizes progress data in the samples according to functional-objectives categories. Again, no strikingly large and significant patterns emerge. However, the progress ratings for the categories tend to show the same relative relationship to the overall mean in both samples. Education objectives are seen as the most difficult to achieve, followed by social objectives. Health and employment objectives appear to be more easily achieved. The two samples differ somewhat in their rating of control objectives.

These two tables suggest that client progress on objectives, as rated by the officers, may be a different phenomenon in the two samples. This indication is not entirely surprising. Progress ratings are influenced to some degree by socioenvironmental conditions, especially for employment and social objectives. The fact that the jurisdiction of Big City is relatively small and geographically well defined while the Eastern Suburbs sample comprises five separate court jurisdictions may account for some differences. In the latter sample, differences in environmental conditions may collapse average progress-rating differences.

More important are the kinds of questions these data raise for resource development. For example, the relatively low rate of achievement in education objectives necessarily raises a policy issue. To explore this issue fully, the agency administrator would have to determine the relationship between

Table 7-4
Progress Ratings by Functional Category: Big City and Eastern Suburbs

Functional Category	Percent Achieved		Average Progress Rating		Number of Objectives Rated	
	Big City	Eastern Suburbs	Big City	Eastern Suburbs	Big City	Eastern Suburbs
Employment	35.4	29.5	3.15	3.22	79	112
Education	14.8	19.4	2.33	3.03	27	36
Social	19.0	21.1	2.81	3.09	63	114
Health	35.7	21.5	3.40	3.34	42	130
Control	15.2	30.3	3.12	3.49	66	76
Total	24.9	24.6	3.03	3.25	277	468

Note: Progress was rated on the following scale: achieved = 5; good = 4; some = 3; little = 2; none = 1.

Note: F-tests show no differences between category totals and sample totals at the .01 level.

achieved educational goals and supervision outcomes. If the objectives are found to be related to case outcome, the administrator would then need to investigate the problems that are interfering with achievement of educational supervision objectives. Official school intervention or even new program development might be deemed necessary to deal with the problem. Again, however, numbers are not the final determinant; the data also show a low rate of achievement in employment objectives, and employment might be seen as an alternative target area.

Whatever the administrative response, it is obvious that accessible data on objectives can help both evaluative and planning notions. To complete the planning process, the administrator may want to obtain more detailed information, perhaps investigating the importance ratings of social objectives not being achieved by officers. Perhaps objectives that are frequently rated as being of little importance, have low progress scores, and are unrelated to outcomes ought, as a matter of policy, to be stricken from the supervision process on the grounds that they are unrelated to valid risk-control aims. Those rated critical but not achieved should receive additional attention and, if possible, staff resources.

The priorities for resource planning will change as the patterns of achievement of objectives change. Keeping output data specifically tied to supervision objectives integrates the agency-planning process with the supervision-planning process: the aggregated data from the latter become the information base for the former.

Summary

In this chapter, we have demonstrated how objectives-based case-planning approaches operating at the line level can make community-supervision administration more effective. Some of the greatest advantages of this approach over traditional strategies are the increased flexibility and creativity it provides to administrators through providing better information for decision making.

If administrators are to achieve these benefits, they must realize that in moving toward an objectives-based system they are trying to change a sociotechnical system. They must involve staff in all aspects of developing the new technology, from designing the forms to determining the means for implementing the new changes. This involvement will make staff commitment to the new system sufficiently strong to guarantee that officers will provide accurate and meaningful data.

Precisely because the data are accurate, the administrator can use them for a variety of purposes, including planning, organizing, and evaluation. To illustrate this potential, we discussed applications of the objectives-based case-planning record to information systems, MBO, zero-based budgeting, and resource development. The uses of the data are limited only by the constraints of the environment and the administrator's creativity.

Notes

1. E.L. Trist, "On Socio-Technical Systems," in *The Planning of Change*, ed. Warren G. Bennis, Kenneth D. Benne, and Robert Chin, 2d ed. (New York: Holt, Rinehart and Winston, 1969), p. 269.

2. The prototype of this approach can be found in Frederick Taylor, *The Principles and Methods of Scientific Management* (New York: Harper Row, 1911); a modern variant discussed below is Peter A. Pyhrr, *Zero-Base Budgeting: A Practical Management Tool for Evaluating Expenses* (New York: Wiley, 1973).

3. A prototype for this approach is found in George C. Homans, *The Human Group* (New York: Harcourt, Brace and World, 1950); recent variants are represented by Chris Argyris, *Integrating the Individual and the Organization* (New York: Wiley, 1964); and Rensis Likert, *The Human Organization* (New York: McGraw-Hill, 1967).

4. Marvin R. Weisbord, *Diagnosing Your Organization: A "Six-Box" Learning Exercise* (Wynnewood, Pa.: Organization Research and Development, 1976), p. 3.

5. Ibid., p. 4.

6. Ibid., p. 5.

7. Homans, *The Human Group.*

8. Rensis Likert, "Measuring Organizational Performance," *Harvard Business Review* 36 (1958):42.

9. American Correctional Association, *Manual of Standards for Adult Probation and Parole Field Services* (Rockville, Md.: Commission on Accreditation for Corrections, 1977).

10. Frederick Herzberg, *Work and the Nature of Man* (New York: World, 1966).

11. Robert Chin and Kenneth Benne, "General Strategies for Effecting Changes in Human Systems," in Bennis, Benne, and Chin, *The Planning of Change*, p. 35.

12. Ibid., p. 39.

13. Todd R. Clear, internal staff memorandum, Model Probation and Parole Systems Project, National Institute of Corrections, Washington, D.C., 1981.

14. Chin and Benne, "General Strategies for Effecting Changes," p. 56.

15. Chris Argyris, *Intervention Theory and Method: A Behavioral Science View* (Reading, Mass.: Addison-Wesley, 1970), p. 105.

16. Paul Hersey and Kenneth Blanchard, *Management of Organizational Behavior: Utilizing Human Resources*, 3d ed. (Englewood Cliffs, N.J.: Prentice-Hall, 1977), p. 126.

17. Warren G. Bennis, *Organizational Development: Its Nature, Origins, and Prospects* (Reading, Mass.: Addison-Wesley, 1969), p. 13.

18. Argyris, *Intervention Theory and Method*, p. 30.

19. Robert Tannenbaum and Frank Massarik, "Participation by Subordinates in the Managerial Decision-Making Process," in *People and Productivity*, ed. Robert A. Sutermeister, 3d ed. (New York: McGraw-Hill, 1976), p. 365.

20. Chris Argyris, *Interpersonal Competence and Organizational Effectiveness* (Homewood, Ill.: Dorsey Press, 1962).

21. Likert, *The Human Organization*, pp. 4-10.

22. C. West Churchman, *The Systems Approach* (New York: Dell, 1968), p. 108.

23. David Duffee, *Correctional Policy and Prison Organization* (New York: Halsted Press, 1975), p. 108.

24. Ibid., p. 194.

25. Ibid., p. 196.

26. Naomi I. Brill, *Teamwork: Working Together in the Human Services* (Philadelphia: Lippincott, 1976), p. 11.

27. Peter F. Drucker, *The Practice of Management* (New York: Harper & Row, 1954).

28. William E. Reif and Gerald Bassford, "What MBO Really Is: Results Require a Complete Program," *Business Horizons*, June 1973, p. 1. Copyright 1973 by the Foundation for the School of Business at Indiana University. Reprinted by permission.

29. Ibid., p. 3.

30. George Odiorne, *Management by Objectives: A System of Managerial Leadership* (New York: Pitman, 1965), p. 78.

31. See Mark L. McConkie, *Management by Objectives: A Corrections Perspective* (Washington, D.C.: U.S. Department of Justice, 1975).

32. Ibid., p. 4.

33. Ibid.

34. Melvyn C. Raider, "A Social Service Model of Management by Objectives," *Social Casework* 58 (1976):525.

35. Ibid.

36. John W. Humble, *How to Manage by Objectives* (New York: American Management Association, 1973).

37. Pyhrr, *Zero-Base Budgeting*.

38. Ibid., p. 6.

39. Ibid., p. xi.

40. Ibid., p. 34.

41. The complete objectives ratings from these interviews are presented in Todd R. Clear, *A Model for Supervising the Offender in the Community* (Washington, D.C.: National Institute of Corrections, 1978).

42. Vincent O'Leary, Todd R. Clear, and James Fox, "Probationer Needs Assessment," mimeographed (Final report, State University of New York, School of Criminal Justice, Albany, 1975), p. 14.

43. Ibid., p. 8.

44. Ibid., p. 22.

45. Ibid.

46. Daniel Glaser, *Routinizing Evaluation: Getting Feedback on the Effectiveness of Crime and Delinquency Programs* (Rockville, Md.: National Institute of Mental Health, Center for Studies of Crime and Delinquency, 1973).

47. Ibid., p. 22.

48. Ibid., p. 105.

49. Ibid., p. 104.

50. Ibid., p. 110.

51. Ibid., p. 111.

52. Richard Galbraith, "Systematic Operational Programs Evaluation" (Paper presented at the meeting of the American Society of Criminology, Tucson, November 1976).

8 Conclusion

The primary aim of community supervision of the offender should be to control the risk that the offender represents by methods that are not unnecessarily intrusive. Any attempt to pursue risk control entails reducing and, if possible, eliminating unwarranted exercise of supervision discretion. One way to do this is to have officers assign clients to risk-control priority levels (classification) and to require that specific supervision objectives be established for each client. Objectives setting provides supervisors with a meaningful tool for controlling line-officer discretion and provides administrators with a data base for conducting short- and long-range program planning and evaluation.

This system borrows extensively from other professional settings, including public administration (systems/planning), education, clinical psychology (prediction), and legal philosophy. Readers familiar with community supervision will also recognize parallels in the operation of many agencies. For example, computerized management-information systems are becoming more common; line staff are frequently asked to indicate their treatment objectives; and no community-supervision agency can reasonably afford to neglect community-protection concerns. What, then, is unique about our model?

Two principal differences exist between our system and common practice in corrections. One is that it attempts to eliminate fragmentation of methods by providing a purposeful superstructure for selecting and evaluating activities. A focus on risk control is a valuable component of such an attempt. Most methods commonly used in community supervision are fragmented in the sense that, although they may be justified for particular clients, they are not useful in relation to all clients. For example, screening for client risk (and need) is becoming more commonplace, but the need for coherent programmatic results from such assessments is often ignored. Instead, there is often a tendency simply to mandate more intensive supervision for higher-risk cases.[1] This type of approach raises more policy questions than it resolves. It is unclear, for example, precisely why high-risk offenders require more-intensive supervision. Is the rationale that these offenders "deserve" more punishment? And how are they to be handled? Should officers simply increase surveillance, or should they provide more services? What standards guide officers' decisions concerning the substance of the intervention? Given the wide variety of officers' approaches to their work, what standards exist to constrain that variety? Most risk-screening systems neglect these issues; they seem to rest the notion that greater risk (which itself is often not defined clearly) automatically requires greater (unspecified) intensity of supervision.

Fragmentation characterizes most existing approaches to supervision-treatment-planning, even those that purport to use objectives. In addition to the fact that the objectives are often poorly written, confusing outcomes with activities, most approaches provide little structure for establishing a given objective. Presumably, an objective is aceptable as long as an officer believes it to be necessary because it is related to a client need. This reasoning shows little sensitivity to the moral issues inherent in coercive social control or to the subjectivity inherent in treatment planning. The result is that tools such as treatment-planning, risk-screening, and information systems often remain fragmented in application, since they are linked to no general overriding agency purposes. Instead of requiring that the result justify the technology used, these systems too often allow the technology to determine the unarticulated goals eventually pursued: risk is assessed because the instrument to do so is available; objectives are written because they are required; managers get information because records have been computerized. Workers may in fact benefit from these systems in various ways, but it is unlikely that the work of community supervision has changed much, except on the surface.

Our approach is based on the notion that a new technology is appropriate only when it is specifically helpful in linking practices and organizational goals. Once we had identified risk control as our mission, we were able to establish a framework for assessing the supervision requirements of a case in terms of both intensity and substance. We determined the constraints that a risk-control model imposes on officers, and we emphasized the importance of making supervision decisions congruent with organizational goals. We have attempted to construct a constellation of focused methods to replace the current fragmentation in supervision. Under our model, risk assessment, case planning, and information systems have a clear relation to orgnizational goals.

The second way in which our system differs from other reform efforts that it focuses on changing the way officers do their work. We approached this difficult problem of change by involving line officers in the design and implementation of the model. We learned that it is relatively simple to implement new paperwork to meet classification and management-information requirements. It is much more difficult to use this paperwork as a vehicle for altering the decisions of staff about cases rather than for merely formalizing the criteria for decisions. This is an important distinction. New procedures do not automatically create new ways of working, and too often administrative change efforts ignore this fact. We believe that a key to actually changing the worker is to allow the change to derive from an analysis of the work itself and to involve the staff in that analysis. Consequently, we have developed an organic model for changing community-supervision practice in which a key element was the change *process* and not simply the product.

The result has been an approach that attempts to balance the tendencies toward mystification and toward demystification in supervision. It attempts to reconcile the view that quality supervision is a product of the intangibles of officer experience and instruction, which cannot be taught but must be learned on the job, with the view that supervision has virtually no impact on offenders and is simply an unwarranted intrusion into the lives of criminals. Our experience, based on this research, inclines us to seek a middle ground. Supervision is an appropriate risk-control sanction that can perform some functions more effectively—and more appropriately—than any existing alternative sanction. To manage the offender in the community requires an open-systems approach in which the objectives of supervision are continually clarified. Feedback serves as a basic tool at all levels of the organization so that the agency as a whole will benefit from the experiences of officers and clients. This is the essence of viewing the organization in socio-technical terms.

By maintaining the importance of a socio-technical approach, we are also supporting the need for continual reassessment of community supervision, with the expectation that adaptations will occur to reflect new knowledge. The materials presented here are based on the results of applied research efforts that took an organic approach to knowledge about supervision. We suspect that future attempts that adopt this process will produce important new improvements for the community-supervision function.

Note

1. See General Accounting Office, *Probation and Parole Activities Need to Be Better Managed* (Washington, D.C.: Government Printing Office, 1977); and American Correctional Association, *Manual of Standards for Adult Probation and Parole Field Services* (Rockville, Md.: Commission on Accreditation for Corrections, 1977).

Appendix A
Program Plan Profile:
Probation Form I

School of Criminal Justice
State University of New York at Albany

_____

(Name of person Completing)

_____

(date Completed)

I. Background Data

The Program Plan Profile is designed to help the probation officer and his agency gain an accurate picture of the needs of probationers and the resources required to meet those needs. To be of greatest use, the Profile Form must be filled out carefully with each step completed before the next is attempted. It takes some time to complete a Profile Form at first, but with some practice the time required decreases considerably.

As a start and in order to make it possible later to classify probationers' needs and resources according to important background characteristics, please complete the brief background statement below.

Probationer Name and/or Number: _____

City or Area of Residence: _____

Date placed on probation: _____ Date case termination: _____

Types of case (delinquent, adult misdemeanant, etc.) _____

Sex: Male _____ Female _____ Age at nearest birthday: _____

Ethnic: __ White __ Black __ Puerto Rican __ Other (specify) _____

Number of prior police contacts (arrests*): _____

Number of prior court contacts (convictions*): _____

Present offense (behavior): _____

_____

Comments: _____

_____

_____

---

*Count multiple arrests and/or convictions stemming from a single incident as one arrest or conviction.

II. Case Analysis

Before proceeding to develop the profile of the resources needed, an analysis of important factors in this individual's situation is needed. In order to help in the task, Kurt Lewin's force-field analysis can be used as a way to picture the situation. Of critical importance to probation services are those forces which bear a strong relationship to the probability of future law violations. In all probationers, combinations of relevant forces exist; those driving him toward law violations as well as those that act to resist further illegal behavior. These forces can be of many kinds. Some forces might be "inside" the probationer as a tendency to cope with frustrating situations by physically assaulting behavior. Still other important forces might be considered "outside" the probationer, as financial troubles or a positive home environment.

In the present situation, we are interested in critical and significant forces which are affecting this client's ability to complete probation and his likelihood of law-abiding behavior—both positive and negative forces, both "inside" and "outside" forces. On the next page is provided a blank force-field. Please fill it in with those significant forces that are related to future illegal activity that you have observed in your contact with this probationer. A completed force-field should allow for a well-rounded picture of this probationer in regard to his law-abiding conduct.

Force-Field

Forces Driving for Law-Abiding Behavior	Forces Resisting (Driving against) Law-Abiding Behavior

III. Identifying Critical Forces

The many forces listed in the force-field analysis offer a variety of points on which to undertake a program of change. Realistically, most programs of change must limit themselves to a relatively small number of items to maintain focus and conserve precious energy and resources. The next step in developing the Plan Profile for this client is to choose a limited number of forces to deal with. Some of the forces you described in the analysis are more critical than others. Some may involve crisis situations in need of immediate solution; others may be centrally related to law-abiding activity. Things to look for in selecting forces for change are:

Strength – identify the strongest forces; those which play a large part in influencing future law-abiding activity.

Alterability – identify forces which you have or you can obtain the skills or resources to assist the probationer to change.

Speed – look for forces which can be worked on immediately and which will have short-range positive effect.

Interdependency – identify those forces which are core forces in the sense that change in these will have influence on a number of other forces.

Critical Forces

List below those specific forces in the force-field analysis that are most critical; those that will be the focus of your change efforts.

IV. Initial Classification*

In developing a Profile it is important to get some information about the amount of agency intervention which is required in a case. Therefore please classify this client according to the estimated degree of intervention called for in this case. Definitions are provided to aid in this initial classification; check that category which in your judgments best applies.

_____ Intensive   (Client recently assigned to probation with a history of violent behavior against others, or he is likely to commit a fairly serious violation of the law or there is high public interest in this case or the requirements imposed by the court can be enforced only by very close and persistent supervision.)

_____ Regular   (Client does not now pose a significant threat to the public and he does not require close supervision because of a specific condition imposed by the court; however, he is currently coping with a significant set of problems, specifically related to potential violations of the law which the client has some expectation of overcoming with the assistance of the probationer service.)

_____ Minimum   (Client does not now pose a significant threat to the public, no requirements of the court call for close supervision and he does not face any important problems which are specifically related to potential serious violations of the law and which the probation services can reasonably expect to affect substantially.)

*These category definitions are adapted from the definitions presented in chapter 4. The differences illustrate how a supervision agency can modify the objectives-specification approach to fit its own situation.

V. Behavioral Objectives

The next step in developing a Profile is to translate the crucial forces listed earlier into behavioral objectives. The goal is to express the outcome desired in terms of some type of behavior. Thus "improved attitudes toward authority" might be expressed as "reduce frequency of arguments with father" or "reduce frequency of arguments with employer." In some cases it may be necessary to use two or more behavioral measures to express the important dimensions of the behavior being sought. In other cases a single behavioral objective may be sufficient.

For each of the crucial forces, list the behavioral objective or objectives which are being sought. Be as specific as you can. For example, you might want the probationer to "attend school regularly with no more than four absences a month."

To aid in specification, please number each objective. In some cases you may wish to break up an objective into several sub-objectives in which case letters would be used. For example, you may wish to break down an objective such as "1 – hold a steady job" into 1a – complete satisfactorily a vocational training course" and "1b - report to work regularly and on time." Use the next page to outline the behavioral objectives for each of the critical forces listed.

After each objective (or sub-objective) has been listed, indicate how important that particular objective is to the outcome of this case. Place a check in the appropriate column on the left of the page.

A check in the column labeled "Court" indicates that the particular objective was specifically ordered by the court as a special condition of probation. Even if this column is checked go ahead and rate the current importance of the objective.

Importance

Critical	*Very*	*Quite*	*Some*	*Little*	*Behavioral Objectives*

VI. Resources Needed to Achieve Objectives

In order to achieve the behavioral objectives listed on the previous page, certain resources or services will need to be brought to bear. For example, in order to aid a drug addict, methadone maintenance might be necessary; to reduce arguments with a father peer group counseling may be needed; and to hold regular employment a job as a mechanic may be needed. Please record on the left side of the page the kind of services or resources that will be necessary to achieve the behavioral objectives indicated on the prior page.

Be as specific as you can. For example, you may believe that, in order to achieve a behavioral objective, some change in attitude is called for and the primary vehicle for this change would be a group experience. In that case try to detail the focus of the group as much as possible. One might ask how a group experience will help achieve the objectives. Peer group counseling for a value change might be more indicated than a psychotherapeutic group experience which aimed at dealing with deeper emotional problems. Other needed services may be more concrete, for example, obtaining some financial support at least temporarily.

For each numbered behavioral objective on the previous page, a resource should be listed here. Thus, objective number 1 on the previous page should be paired with its corresponding resource on the next page.

In the righthand column indicate the resource you will actually use to achieve each objective. In the case of a job need, a state employment service might be listed. Each resource actually used should be numbered to correspond with each resource needed. For example, you may have broken a single objective into several sub-objectives (1a, 1b, 1c, etc.) For each sub-objective you should list the resource needed and the resource actually being used to achieve that objective.

After you have listed a resource needed and being used for each objective and sub-objective, you should rate the utility of that resource by judging its usefulness for achieving that particular related behavioral objective. If the resource needed to achieve the objective is not available, *and* nothing is being used to achieve the objective, write "not available" in the second column of the page under "resources used." Otherwise, write specifically the resource being used for the objective and rate its utility for the particular objective.

		Usefulness of Resource		
Resources Needed to Achieve Objectives	*Resources Used to Achieve Objectives*	*Good*	*Fair*	*Poor*

Appendix B
Henry Ward Case

State of Jefferson
Department of Corrections
Jefferson State Reformatory

Initial Probation Report

Date: March 27, 1970

Name: Henry Ward   No.: 187,364

Date Sentenced: 3/10/70   Offense: Assault second degree

Sentence: Probation - 3 years

Age: 17   Sex: M   Birthplace: Dallas, Texas   Race: Caucasian

Citizenship: U.S.   Marital Status: Single   Education Status: 9th grade

Prior Record

Date	Place	Offense	Disposition
5/6/66	Ramsey, Mo.	Larceny of Auto driving without permit	Probation - 1 year; fined $35
4/29/67	Ramsey, Mo.	Probation Violation	Probation extended 1 year
11/5/68	Central City, Jefferson	Speeding	
1/10/69	Central City, Jefferson	No reverse gear, no hand brakes, no rear license tags	Handled in Juvenile Court Driver's permit suspended and restored in 90 days
1/69	Illinois	Trespassing on farmer's property	Informal probation, provided he remain out of Tooker County, Illinois

Current Offense

Defendants Ward and Duke, on or about October 13, 1969 (1:25 A.M.), in Central City, State of Jefferson, purposely and with deliberate and premediated malice did assault one Arthur Kemp. The case of assault first degree was dismissed November 8, 1969, in the District Court after juvenile court waived jurisdiction October 25, 1969. Ward was convicted of assault second degree and sentenced to three years' probation. Duke was similarly convicted and sentenced.

Inmate's Version

Trouble started when Kemp, a coworker with subject, cared to find Joe Fisher. Subject and Duke refused to let Kemp get to Fisher, who was asleep in his apartment. Kemp thought that Fisher had given his girlfriend liquor on which she had gotten drunk. A fight ensued in which subject was hit with brass knuckles. Kemp went away but later returned and started another fight, kicking Duke, which necessitated hospitalization and an operation on his eye. Police arrested Kemp and Duke for disturbing the peace. Kemp was reported drunk.

A few days later, Kemp sent a message to subject and Duke that if he next saw them anywhere he was going to kill them. Subject states he stayed away from work to avoid Kemp. About a week later, subject and Duke were followed in their car by the victim and taunted about being afraid to fight. That night subject and Duke went to another friend's home, where subject picked up "some beer," and drove by victim's girlfriend's home, where victim was living at the time. Seeing Kemp's car parked there, they stopped; Duke jumped out and called to the victim to come out. When Kemp came out, subject and Duke proceeded to "beat him up." (Kemp suffered severe lacerations, which required two days of hospitalization.) Subject took off in the middle of the fight and was on his way home but was apprehended before he arrived. Duke ran away and slept in a garage until the next day, when he gave himself up. They were charged with first-degree assault but were allowed instead to plead guilty to second-degree assault, which they did.

Home and Family History

Subject was born in Dallas, Texas, in June 1952. The family moved to Missouri in 1954. His father was a flier in the navy and traveled a great deal. Subject attended schools in Ramsey, Missouri, and in Arizona to the seventh grade, states he did well until he got into the junior high school.

His parents were divorced soon after his birth (1957); his father remarried sometime in 1958; his mother never remarried. Subject has lived with her and his grandmother all his life, except for two years with his father in

Arizona. He went there in 1963 and returned to Missouri in 1965. Subject claims that his mother sent him to Arizona because of some trouble he had gotten into. After he had been in Arizona a year, a judge got in touch with his father and placed him in his father's custody for another year. He returned to Missouri in 1965 and did not report to the court official again. About eighteen months later (approximately 1966) he got into some trouble (auto theft) and spent a year on probation. After this his mother took him to Memphis, where she went to look for work. They were there about three weeks in 1967, returned to Missouri, then came to Central City in September 1967. His mother found a job at Court's Department Store, worked there for about six months, then went to work for Central City Hospital as an electrocardiogram operator. She is a trained physiotherapist. Subject currently lives with his mother.

School History

The defendant received most of his schooling in Missouri. He has a poor record of attendance and was considered a serious behavior problem. He was suspended from the high school in Ramsey for poor behavior, and the school psychiatrist recommended him for enrollment in a special school for problem boys. His mother was uncooperative with the authorities and refused to send him, but instead placed him in a private boarding school in Missouri (Kirk's Academy). He was expelled after two weeks for very unstable behavior, absences, and lack of cooperation. He was considered to be "insecure and mixed up." He was then enrolled in the Small School after considerable pressure on his mother but was again removed when his mother moved away from Ramsey, apparently to get away from legal pressures to keep him in school. She had been cooperating in his lateness to classes and his absences from school because she did not want him in Small. No other school in Ramsey would accept him, so she tried Jonesville, Missouri, where he entered Jonesville High School in 1967. He did very poorly in his studies, truanted and associated with undesirables, and was constantly getting into trouble with the authorities, including the police, for insubordination. The mother and son always claimed that they were being "picked on." Subject states that "an education helps" but believes that he can "make it" without finishing school.

Employment History

Ward was employed as a truck driver, a grillman, and a gas-station attendant during the latter part of 1968 and, intermittently, for short periods (not over five months) during 1969. He falsified his age to obtain one job driving a wrecker. In all cases he lost the jobs for reasons that he claims were not his fault.

In one instance, he claims he was not being paid; in another, he was transferred to another place too far to go without a car; and in another, he was afraid to go back to his job because of a fight with the fellow worker, the victim of the assault.

He is unskilled and inexperienced in any kind of work and is currently unemployed. His longest work experience is five months as a grillman in a restaurant. Subject states that he likes driving a truck and hopes to get his license back so that he can return to that job.

Psychological Evaluation

Ward is an individual of at least high-average intelligence whose academic progress has been adversely affected by the early development of behavior difficulties so severe as to disrupt completely his previous school adjustment. Schooling might be attempted, with emphasis on numerical skills.

Ward is the victim of a broken and nomadic home. He feels rejected by his father, who has remarried successfully and has two children by his second wife. Ward is the only child of his mother's only marriage and is overprotected, overindulged, and victimized generally by his mother's apparently poor judgment. She has intervened in his behalf with the police, courts, schools, and correctional institutions in a most destructive and short-sighted manner, to the point that it can be said that she has become a primary cause and support of the inmate's delinquent behavior.

Insofar as the circumstances surrounding the present situation are concerned, Ward has told various tales, none of which coincides particularly well with the official version, and all of which differ in important essentials from one another. His primary effort appears to be the minimization of his own obviously intimate involvement in the entire affair. He impresses me as an impulsive young delinquent who is inclined to alter facts in order to present himself in the most-favorable light. He is quite defensive and holds markedly asocial feelings and attitudes toward society in general and authority in particular. He is emotionally constricted, socially withdrawn, and personally conflicted. His defenses are almost infantile in their crudeness, archaism, and ineffectuality. He evaluates himself as "friendly, strict in his dealings with others, quiet, and competent," but in the next breath admits his explosive temper, feeling of tenseness, and inability to manipulate his environment successfully enough.

Religious Report

Henry is a member of the Catholic church, having been baptized in the State of Texas in his early childhood. He has received the basic Catholic teachings.

During his confinement at the Central City Jail, he became very friendly with Father Brown, the chaplain there at the time, and renewed his interest in the faith. He has been very faithful in attendance at Mass every Sunday.

Prior Performance on Probation

Subject was on probation for two years, from ages thirteen to fifteen. His probation officer was Emily Loucks of the Marion County, Missouri, Juvenile Court. He was verbal and cooperative, initially responding well to probation counseling. While on probation he was involved in group counseling, which he seemed to enjoy. However, most of his cooperation was seen as superficial, aimed primarily at making a good impression on the probation officer. He often would give verbal agreement to the probation officer's directives, then ignore them after leaving the office. Later he would again apologize for his rule-breaking behavior.

Subject was found to be in violation of probation as a result of expulsion from school.

Health

Subject appears to be in good general health, with the exception of seriously decayed and unsightly teeth; otherwise his appearance is attractive. Subject smokes more than two packs of cigarettes a day and admits to frequent drinking to the point of drunkenness (subject says he has "passed out" more than once while drunk). He also admits to sporadic use of marijuana but says he has never tried hard drugs and is afraid to experiment with them.

Financial Status

Since he has been unemployed, Wade has had little money but appears to need little. His mother provides his room and board and gives him spending money "whenever he needs it."

Present Situation

Subject is currently living with his mother. The father is in Arizona, a flier in the air force, remarried, and has two children. His grandmother and grandfather are divorced, with the grandfather in Chicago, the grandmother in Ramsey working for the city. He claims about fifty cousins and more aunts and uncles scattered over the country, none of whom are close. There seems to be a close relationship between subject and his mother, a trained physiotherapist, who has already shown a great interest in his situation.

Subject is not married but has had a "steady" girlfriend for the last year, with whom he admits having sexual relations. This relationship appears to present some problems. The girl, Diane Werblin, age seventeen, is still in school. Her parents do not approve of her relationship with subject and "do everything they can" to thwart it. Apparently there have been some nasty arguments between subject and the girl's father.

Subject spends a good deal of time with his friends, some of whom are also unemployed. They seem to spend much of their time "drinking beer and driving around."

Index

177

About the Authors

Todd R. Clear is assistant professor at the School of Criminal Justice, Rutgers University. He received the B.A. from Anderson College, Indiana, and the M.A. and Ph.D. from the State University of New York at Albany. He has served as a consultant to numerous probation and parole agencies around the country through various projects funded by the National Institute of Corrections, including the Case Management Institutes and the Model Probation and Parole Systems Project; and he is a consultant to the New York City Department of Probation's Differential Supervision Project. He is coauthor of *Corrections: An Issues Approach* and *Sentencing By Mathematics: An Evaluation of Sentencing Guidelines in Three Courts*, as well as numerous articles and papers on criminal justice and corrections.

Vincent O'Leary is currently president of the State University of New York at Albany. He received the B.A. from San Francisco State University and completed his graduate training in sociology at the University of Washington. He served as the assistant director of the President's Commission on Law Enforcement and Administration of Justice and was a consultant to the National Commission on the Causes and Prevention of Violence. He was appointed by the U.S. attorney general to the National Advisory Panel on Law Enforcement Education, and served as director of the National College for Juvenile Court Judges at the University of Nevada. He is currently editor of the *Journal of Research in Crime and Delinquency*, director of the National Parole Institutes, and a member of the Board of Editors of the *Journal of Offender Rehabilitation*. His publications include numerous monographs and articles on criminal justice and corrections.